After Tiananmen Square: Challenges for the Chinese-American Relationship

Jürgen Domes
Chen Qimao
Harlan W. Jencks
Douglas Pike
Ding Xinghao
Robert L. Pfaltzgraff, Jr.

**Special Report
1990**

A Publication of the
INSTITUTE FOR FOREIGN POLICY ANALYSIS, INC.
Cambridge, Massachusetts, and Washington, D.C.

BRASSEY'S (US), Inc.
Maxwell Macmillan Pergamon Publishing Corp.

Washington New York London Oxford
Beijing Frankfurt Sao Paulo Sydney Tokyo Toronto

Brassey's (US), Inc., Press Offices:

U.S.A. (Editorial)	Brassey's (US), Inc. 8000 Westpark Drive, 4th floor, McLean, Virginia 22102 USA
(Orders)	Attn: Order Dept., Macmillan Publishing Company Front and Brown Streets, Riverside, NJ 08075
U.K. (Editorial)	Brassey's (UK) Ltd. 50 Fetter Lane, London EC4A 1AA England
(Orders)	Brassey's (UK) Ltd. Headington Hill Hall, Oxford OX3 0BW, England
PEOPLE'S REPUBLIC OF CHINA	Pergamon Press, Room 4037, Qianmen Hotel, Beijing People's Republic of China
FEDERAL REPUBLIC OF GERMANY	Pergamon Press GmbH, Hammerweg 6, D-6242 Kronberg, Federal Republic of Germany
BRAZIL	Pergamon Editora Ltda, Rua Eça de Queiros, 346 CEP 04011, Paraiso, São Paulo, Brazil
AUSTRALIA	Brassey's Australia, P.O. Box 544 Potts Point, N.S.W. 2011, Australia
JAPAN	Pergamon Press, 5th Floor, Matsuoka Central Building 1-7-1 Nishishinjuku, Shinjuku-ku, Tokyo 160, Japan
CANADA	Pergamon Press Canada, Suite No. 271, 253 College Street Toronto, Ontario, Canada M5T 1R5

Brasseys (US), Inc., books are available at special discounts for bulk purchases for sales, promotions, premiums, fund-raising, or educational use through the Special Sales Director, Macmillan Publishing Company, 866 Third Avenue, New York, NY 10022.

Library of Congress Cataloging-in-Publication Data

After Tiananmen Square: challenges for the Chinese-American
relationship/Jürgen Domes . . [et al.].

      p. cm.—(Special report)
      "A Publication of the Institute for Foreign Policy Analysis, Inc."
      ISBN 0-08-040559-2: $9.95
1. United States—Foreign relations—China. 2. China—Foreign relations—United States.
3. United States—Foreign relations—1989- 4. China—Foreign relations—1976-
I. Domes, Jürgen. II. Institute for Foreign Policy Analysis. III. Series: Special
report (Institute for Foreign Policy Analysis)

E183.8.C5A64   1990
327.73051—dc20   90-2697
                                          CIP

First Printing 1990

Printed by Corporate Press, Inc., Landover, Maryland.

Contents

Preface

In the 1990s, the United States faces a rapidly unfolding security environment in the Asian-Pacific area. Its principal features are familiar: the economic dynamism of market economies; the growth of representative institutions in the Republic of Korea; steps toward the establishment of diplomatic relations between Japan and, respectively, China and the Soviet Union; the impact of China's internal policies on relations with outside powers, especially the United States; and the implications of the Persian Gulf crisis for Asian-Pacific countries, especially Japan, to mention the most obvious.

For nearly a generation the United States has been in the process of evolving with the People's Republic of China a relationship based on the importance attached to China as a vitally important component of U.S. strategy and the global and regional power balance from the early 1970s to the late 1980s. Across successive American Administrations, Sino-American relations appeared to be established on a course that was leading to a thickening web of contacts and other interactive patterns—a process that was directly affected by the tragic events of Tiananmen Square in June 1989.

This Special Report was designed to provide an assessment of the implications of the Tiananmen Square massacre for Sino-American relations in the 1990s; in a broader sense to set forth for the United States a range of perspectives related to China's domestic politics, global strategies, and regional policies with a focus on the Western Pacific and Southeast Asia; and last but not least, to provide a series of implications and policy options for the Sino-American relationship.

This work is published as part of a series of studies on the Eurasian rimlands in which the Institute for Foreign Policy Analysis has been engaged. Their purpose is to survey the strategic setting, as well as the policies and prospects of individual states, in regions of vital importance to the United States. Such an exercise is essential as the United States develops its policy priorities for the 1990s leading toward and beyond the end of this century.

We express thanks to the J. Howard Pew Freedom Trust for support to the Institute for Foreign Policy Analysis that made possible this project and publication of this Special Report.

Robert L. Pfaltzgraff, Jr.
President
Institute for Foreign Policy Analysis

Executive Summary

China's Internal Dynamics in the 1990s

From April 17 through June 3, 1989, first tens of thousands and ultimately millions of Chinese—initially, mainly university students, but increasingly, people from all walks of life among the urban population—held demonstrations in Beijing and at least sixteen other Chinese cities, demanding human rights, freedom, and democracy. From May 4 through June 3, demonstrators occupied the very center of China's capital, Tiananmen Square, established their own autonomous organizations and unions, policed major parts of Beijing, and began to develop spontaneously their own administrative networks.

In the early morning hours of June 4, units of the Chinese armed forces—the People's Liberation Army (PLA)—moved in with tanks, armored personnel carriers, and other weapons, swiftly suppressing the movement and killing between 2,500 and 8,000 citizens in Beijing alone, most of whom were unarmed. Starting on June 6, the Chinese Communist Party (CCP) launched a nationwide campaign to wipe out the pro-democracy movement, arresting some 20,000 people and executing at least 29 participants during the month of June alone.

These events have dramatically changed the domestic political scene in the PRC. After the Spring Crisis of 1989, the optimistic projections about China's future that had been advanced by a host of statesmen, politicians, businessmen, and journalists in almost all Western countries could no longer be sustained. They had contended that the policies of economic reform and of opening to the outside world, enacted by the ruling elite since 1978, had become "irreversible," and that the country appeared to be moving toward domestic political openness if not democracy.

Indeed, the policies of economic reform, in the ten years from early 1979 to late 1988, had resulted in remarkable success. The average real GNP growth rate for these ten years stood at 8.33 percent annually. Growth rates in grain production and in industry, particularly for light and consumer goods, were impressive. Personal income rose significantly, and the gap between rural and urban income narrowed.

In 1985, however, the first signs that the country was moving into an economic crisis could be detected. This crisis fully manifested itself during 1988, affecting the entire society. For one thing, the economy started to overheat, and inflation became a serious problem in 1988 when the official rate reached 18.5 percent; in fact, the real inflation rate in 1988 was probably between 30 and 35 percent. By May 1989 the official rate was up to 27 percent. The dramatic price increases primarily affected industrial workers, teachers and professors, and the intelligentsia. It also affected cadres in the party and the bureaucracy, which led to an increase in bribery, embezzlement, and other forms of corruption that soon permeated the governmental structure to an unprecedented degree.

These signs of increasing economic and social decay were aggravated by the fact that, from the early- to mid-1980s, the Marxist-Leninist doctrine had progressively lost its motivating force for a growing portion of the Chinese populace. The peasants had benefited most from the core element of the economic reform policies that had been enacted by Deng Xiaoping and his associates since 1979, yet their support for the ruling elite was not expressed through political activity, and was not based on a belief in the doctrines of the CCP. Engineers, foremen, and urban workers, too, had profited from the economic reform policies; yet, for them, the impact of inflation gradually eroded their trust in the party and its doctrine, and they started to display a rising propensity toward dissent.

The new private entrepreneurs in the PRC—"self-employed workers" and owners of "individual enterprises"—also profited greatly from the policies of the reform-oriented revisionists within the leadership. They were afraid, however, that a return to stricter socialist doctrines could threaten their livelihood; hence, while supporting the policies of economic reform, they were skeptical about the Marxist-Leninist doctrine.

The most negative attitudes toward party doctrine were to be found among the young people, particularly college and university students. Since the early 1980s, many urban youths and an increasing number of young people in the more affluent village areas have become cynical about Marxism-Leninism. Since 1984, the Chinese media have acknowledged that the youth of the PRC was in the midst of a "crisis of three faiths," that it has no faith in the party, no faith in socialism, and no faith in the fatherland.

In the summer of 1988 the ruling elite, faced with a major economic crisis and the erosion of the legitimating ideology, decided to put the brakes on the policies of economic reform, to strengthen centralized planning, and to institute price ceilings on 326 groups of products. But developments in the winter of 1988-1989 rendered it difficult to implement these new economic policies. Officials in many provinces were hesitant to carry out these policies and some even flatly refused to do so; on the local level, also, obedience to central directives declined significantly.

Hence, the reasons for the Spring Crisis of 1989 become clear: a strong wave of urban discontent with elite policy coinciding with a major intra-elite conflict between the orthodox and the revisionist groups within the leadership. The immediate result of the crisis itself was the violent suppression of the Democracy Movement. The orthodox faction, strengthened by the shift of Deng Xiaoping toward support of its policies, won the intra-elite conflict. Repressive measures by the PRC confirmed the fact that, for the time being, China has moved in the direction of a neo-Stalinist bureaucratic socialism.

For the next few years, we cannot expect the PRC to return to "normalcy." Under the impact of increased repression, the Chinese people will try to circumvent the political system and the demands of the ruling elite to an even greater extent than they have during the last five years. They will increasingly move away from the socialist economic system toward an ever expanding parallel or second economy of moonlighting, black marketeering, illegal exchange of foreign currency, and underground banking and production. This trend is bound to weaken the structures of social control, although those of political control may be strengthened for the immediate future.

The population growth and economic development trends that can be expected for the next decade do not leave much room for optimism from the ruling elite's point of view. The PRC will remain an underdeveloped country with very limited prospects for accelerated modernization through and beyond the end of the twentieth century. Moreover, it is unlikely that, within the next few years, the ruling elite, ridden with political and social problems, will be able to solve the three major economic problems with which the PRC is beset: inflation, energy shortfalls, and shortages of raw and semi-processed materials. Additionally, there is always the possibility of a poor harvest that could cause at least regional famine.

Any effort to forecast possible political trends during the next decade in the PRC must begin with the projection that the ruling elite will be successful in its attempt to stifle dissent, and that this will assure the evolution of a stable system of bureaucratic socialism. In this case, the ruling elite would continue to pursue its policy of a selective and controlled opening toward the outside world, but freeze domestic economic reforms at the 1988 level. Yet the evolution of a stable, institutionalized system of bureaucratic socialism, which means the continuation of Marxist-Leninist single-party rule well into the next century, has, since the Spring Crisis of 1989, become a very shaky foundation on which to build major strategy options for international politics.

The future of communist single-party rule in China is fairly easy to predict: New crises will deepen the rift and sharpen the contradiction between rulers and people, and between party and society. Since June 4, 1989, this gap has become unbridgeable. The outlook for the PRC political system points unmistakably toward a collapse of the communist system, yet it is by no means clear how long Marxist-Leninist rule may last. An examination of the political trends that may develop during the 1990s on the mainland of China can be accomplished through several alternative scenarios.

The first scenario involves a relatively long-term, though fragile, stabilization of the structures of domestic control. This would require a long period of repression under a predominantly orthodox leadership, and the freezing or rolling back to 1988 levels advances made in the areas of individual enterprises, state enterprise autonomy, and decollectivized agricultural production. In order to sustain this repression, the bureaucratic elements of the economy would have to be strengthened. As a consequence, social tensions would increase and eventually explode in manifestations of violent dissent. The ruling elite could probably stifle dissent for the short term, but ultimately the confrontation in China would result in the bloody overthrow of communist rule.

In a second scenario, reform-oriented revisionists would eventually be able to gain control of the decision-making organs of party and state. The new leadership would try to push ahead with thoroughgoing economic reforms, including the decollectivization of rural land-ownership, the lifting of most if not all limitations on individual enterprise, and the granting of broader autonomy to public enterprises. Such daring reforms would be accompanied by political changes: an extension of direct elections to the provincial and ultimately the national level; the granting of considerable autonomy to social organizations; and the introduction of a free choice among several candidates in elections. But the reintroduction of economic and political reforms would in all likelihood result in a demand for further reforms, and this movement would gradually dislodge the party from power—a situation somewhat similar to that in Poland today—and, hence, ensure a comparatively peaceful transition from the communist to a more pluralistic political system.

The third scenario would also witness return of reform-oriented revisionists, who would assume control of the decision-making organs of party and state and start to develop policies of economic and political reform. But in this case these policies would prompt a backlash from orthodox forces, more likely than not in the form of a coup d'etat sanctioned by factions in the PLA. Such a coup would then provoke reaction from society in the form of a nationwide revolutionary movement which, with the support of other factions in the PLA, would finally result in the violent overthrow of communist rule.

It is possible to project a fourth scenario in which a leadership crisis follows the death of Deng Xiaoping, Chen Yun, and other veteran revolutionaries, possibly coupled with a swift aggravation of the current economic crisis. Under these circumstances, which would develop earlier than most observers expect, opposition forces in society would rise again on an even larger scale than they did in the spring of 1989. Faced with this intense opposition, many members of the PLA would no longer be willing to protect the rulers and fight the people, resulting in the disintegration of control structures and the whole system of CCP rule. The transition to another political system would be accomplished without large-scale bloodshed, leaving China under the rule of noncommunist elites well before the end of this century.

Caution should be observed in predicting the unfolding of political dynamics in the PRC during the 1990s and beyond. While the representative democracies throughout the world were impressed by the extent to which the Democracy Movement in the spring of 1989 shared their values, they and their citizens should be aware that the evolution of a democratic political system is not the only alternative to communist rule in China. Nativistic or even atavistic alternatives could develop, which might result in replacing communist totalitarian rule with a totalitarian rule of a different, perhaps fascist or traditionalist, persuasion.

The West should try to keep open as many gates into China as possible without compromising our support for change. It is most important to remember that China as a country is not identical with the current ruling elite of the PRC; the task of Western statesmen must be to devise strategies to continue and deepen our contacts with the forces that will shape the future. If the Western powers concentrate their efforts on this task, they may be able to win the cooperation and even the friendship of twenty-first-century China, and that should be a foremost goal for Western policymakers today.

China's Global Strategic Perspectives on the Third World

In a comparison and analysis of Chinese and U.S. policies toward the Asian-Pacific region, we can find much common ground and many similarities. For instance, their policies are basically the same on Afghanistan, in parallel on other South Asian issues, and close to each other on Kampuchea. On Korea, the two countries adopt different positions: China supports North Korea whereas the United States backs South Korea, but both agree on the issue of maintaining peace and stability in the Korean Peninsula.

Toward the Middle East, Africa, and Central America, however, there exist significant differences. For instance, on the Middle East, China strongly criticizes the United States for its support for Israel and opposition to the PLO. On South Africa, China has strongly criticized American leaders for not putting enough pressure on South African authorities to end racial discrimination. On Central America, for a long time China has opposed U.S. support of the Nicaraguan Contras and its flagrant interference in Nicaragua's internal affairs. On such issues as North-South relations and the establishment of the New International Economic Order, the positions of China and the United States tend to be diametrically opposed.

There are a number of reasons why differences exist between China and the United States on their policies toward the third world. First, they have different points of departure. The United States is a superpower with global interests. Belonging to the third world, China is now preoccupied with socialist modernization and needs a stable, peaceful international environment conducive to its modernization program and good relations with its neighbors. Different points of departure will naturally lead to different policies. As a major third world country and a permanent member of the UN Security Council, China cannot but speak out and uphold what it considers to be justice on certain issues relating to third world countries.

Second, the United States is the leading industrial country whereas China is the largest developing one. The differences in their respective conditions and economic interests will certainly be reflected in their foreign policies.

Third, differences in social systems and ideologies are also reflected in their policies toward the third world. While China emphasizes that state-to-state relations of peaceful coexistence transcend differences in social systems and ideologies, some Americans stress the role of ideology in international relations. American leaders are more apt to use their nation's power indiscreetly to influence internal affairs in third world countries. Applying American values, they try to use these weaker nations to serve America's interests. This is very harmful and naturally repugnant to China and other third world countries.

There are additional factors that influence the third world policies of China and the United States. First, despite the fact that China and the United States have policy differences over a number of issues related to the third world, these two countries have no direct conflict of interests over them. This is because China has no direct interests in the Middle East, Africa, and Central America; China's support to the Arab countries, the PLO, and the black people of South Africa, and so on, is largely moral, not material. The differences between China and the United States on these issues are reflected mainly in the debates at the United Nations and other international bodies. Second, their differences in policies toward the third world, therefore, have not had much impact on U.S.-Chinese bilateral relations. What weakens these relations is not primarily differences in foreign policies, but U.S. interference with China's internal affairs on such issues as Taiwan. Third, in recent years the United States has either made some readjustments (for instance, on South Africa) or is prepared to do so (for instance, on Middle East and Central American issues). Meanwhile, China's own foreign policies, in their implementation, have become increasingly pragmatic and flexible. Consequently, Chinese and U.S. differences in this regard appear to be narrowing.

China pursues independent and peaceful foreign policies. Whether on international or domestic affairs, China will, as always, take positions and measures according to its own judgments and subject to no pressures from the superpowers or groups of big powers. China attaches great importance to Chinese-U.S. relations and holds that the stable development of such relations will not only benefit China and the United States, but also contribute significantly to the maintenance of peace and stability in the world. On third world issues, recognizing its disputes with the United States, China will continue to adhere to the principle of being independent and maintaining its own positions on the one hand, while also seeking common ground and attempting to resolve differences on the other hand, thus preventing these differences from adversely affecting bilateral relations.

China's Evolving Interests in the Western Pacific

In the aftermath of the PRC's suppression of the pro-democracy movement in June 1989, China's international relations are somewhat turbulent, but relations with the Korean states and Southeast Asia have not changed significantly. The already strained relationships with Hong Kong and the rival Republic of China (ROC) on Taiwan are considerably worse. Even more than usual, foreign relations are not receiving the primary attention of Chinese leaders. However, Hong Kong and Taiwan are not exactly "foreign" issues. They are subject to "reunification," an emotive issue among senior PRC leaders.

China has assumed a truly equidistant position between the United States and the Soviet Union in the last year. The main achievement so far of the Soviet "peace offensive" in Asia has been Sino-Soviet detente. Gorbachev essentially fulfilled China's conditions for detente, pulling Soviet forces out of Afghanistan, pressuring Vietnam to withdraw from Cambodia, and promising major troop reductions in the eastern part of the USSR. There will be a significant reduction in Soviet *anti-Chinese* military power, which Moscow will try to use to press for American and Japanese military reductions.

The Republic of Korea's (ROK) emergence as a world trading power, together with the Sino-Soviet detente, broke the status quo in Korea in the mid-1980s. Friendly Sino-American relations facilitated rapid development of PRC-ROK trade. This cooled PRC relations with North Korea, offering an opening to Moscow. In 1984, the Soviets drastically increased military aid to Pyongyang. Increased Soviet influence in Pyongyang is not necessarily a bad thing, since the Russians have a stake in restraining North Korean adventurism. It is good for everybody else in Asia that the Sino-Soviet detente has robbed Kim Il Sung of his ability to play China and the Soviet Union against each other.

The PRC, the Soviet Union, and the United States should avoid complicating the Korean situation by escalating military aid, sales, or commitments. The United States and the ROK need to revise their military relationship, increasing ROK control, and decreasing U.S. troop levels.

The Sino-Soviet detente is a mixed blessing for Taiwan. If Beijing were to decide to use force to "reunify the fatherland," it would be less constrained by the need to defend its northern border. On the other hand, Washington may feel less compelled to consider PRC wishes regarding Taiwan. Sympathy for Taiwan in the United States has been reinforced by revulsion against Beijing's suppression of the pro-democracy movement.

Faced with progressive diplomatic isolation in late 1988, Taipei undertook a new "flexible policy," which includes generous economic aid to its friends. In July 1989, Grenada, which already had diplomatic ties with Beijing, extended recognition to Taipei. It had formal diplomatic relations with both Chinas for eleven days, while PRC diplomats tried to persuade Grenada to reverse its decision. That was tacit recognition that small, poor countries, especially those outside Asia, have little practical reason to stick with Beijing, and may be contemplating the "Grenada model."

Although the legitimacy of the KMT-dominated Republic of China government has been based on the principle that there is only one China, the regime now has substantial domestic support, and may no longer need that legitimating myth. Now is an ideal time for the United States to strengthen quasi-official ties with Taiwan. Faced with Taiwan's increasing prosperity and diplomatic resurgence, and with the long-term possibility of Taiwan independence, Beijing may resort to threat, blockade, or even attempted invasion some time after 1997.

Taiwan's future depends in part upon Hong Kong's fate, which in turn depends upon the PRC's internal political evolution between now and 1997. Beijing has powerful economic and diplomatic incentives to leave Hong Kong's internal social and economic system unchanged. But PRC leaders have overriding political reasons for doing to Hong Kong what they are currently doing to the mainland. If that means throwing out the economic "baby" with the political "bath water," the older generation of Chinese leaders are prepared to do so.

With the failure of the International Conference on Cambodia in Paris in the summer of 1989, the Vietnamese "withdrawal" on September 30 intensified the fighting, which led to limited reintroduction of Vietnamese forces. Further diplomatic progress will await a decisive change in the military situation or an internal political change within one or more of the Khmer parties. In the long run China has more to gain than to lose from peace in Indochina. Any nationalistic Cambodian government, whatever its political complexion, will be traditionally anti-Vietnamese, so there is little practical justification for China's continued backing of the Khmer Rouge. Should the Khmer Rouge regain power, or prevent a peaceful settlement, China will be blamed by the ASEAN states.

The disputed Spratly Island group in the South China Sea is a potential battleground. A comprehensive, multi-national settlement is needed to internationalize and neutralize the Spratlys. Recent South Sea clashes and the increased capability and reach of the Chinese Navy have provoked some alarm in Southeast Asia. Observers throughout the region are especially disturbed by the recent emergence of PRC military doctrine and "rapid reaction forces" for "limited wars." Such a rapid deployment force is alarming to China's neighbors because it can form the basis of an offensive power projection capability.

China's Policies Toward Vietnam and Cambodia

Sino-Vietnamese relations are best viewed in socio-psychological terms. There is an ancient association, one that has always been exceedingly complex. For the Vietnamese, China and its Confucian values are at the core of Vietnamese identity; Vietnam's very existence, historically and today, is intricately bound up with China. Nothing much ever will—ever *can*—change this basic association. China will always dominate Vietnam in a thousand psychological ways and the Vietnamese will always deny this. Vietnam, as self-preservation, will resist each Chinese advance, even those with the best of Chinese motives.

What is now under way between the two is a redefining of the relationship. This process is more significant than are the various outstanding finite problems. The Vietnamese seek an end to the old pupil-*sensei* relationship. However, they acknowledge that in the long run they must get along with China, which means accommodating Chinese interests. It is a slow process which could take a decade or more to complete. To a considerable extent the final outcome will turn on the generational transfer of power to new leaders in Hanoi. For the Vietnamese, workable relations with China is not a matter of whether, but of how and when.

Outsider analyses of Sino-Vietnamese relations over the years has tended to be simplistic. Either the central issue was China's effort to turn Vietnam into a satellite and its willingness to use naked force if required; or it was the centripetal force pressing Vietnam away from China toward permanent implacability. They were oil and water, or were forever big and little dragon. Some held the only important consideration was the historic Vietnamese fear and hatred of China. Others drew parallels to the Soviet-Finnish relationship. None of these has proved accurate enough to be useful. Rather they represent the sort of thinking that must be discarded if we are ever to see clearly the nature of the relationship or predict correctly its future course.

Sino-Vietnamese relations began in the late 1980s a slow warming process, one that can be expected to continue into the 1990s, although probably at the same glacial speed that has marked the previous decade. The major finite issue between them—PAVN occupation of Cambodia—may be close to resolution. Hanoi will probably distance itself from Moscow somewhat in the next decade, since it appears to be in the interests of all parties that this happen. The Vietnamese dream of a Federation of Indochina has been put on hold, at least temporarily, and it could be dropped altogether given a new and younger leadership in Hanoi with a different set of priorities. The Sino-Vietnamese dispute over the offshore islands gives no indication of being resolved soon, perhaps not even in the 1990s. Nor has China signaled an intent to change its basic policy approach toward Vietnam—pursuing what the Vietnamese call the "multifaceted war of sabotage"—the military, economic and diplomatic effort to "bleed" Vietnam in Cambodia, to undermine its economic development efforts, and to vilify it in international diplomatic forums, making Hanoi's "independent" behavior as costly as possible. Eventually this policy probably will change. Based on past Chinese behavior, when it does change it will come abruptly and with little forewarning.

It seems clear that eventually, perhaps beyond the 1990s, there will be a rapprochement between Vietnam and China, because such a development would clearly benefit both parties. However, beyond formal Confucian harmony, there will always be limits to rapprochement, since it is inevitable that future regional balance of power politics will dictate that, in pursuit of their own national interests, these two countries will always be in competition.

A Chinese Perspective on Sino-U.S. Relations

Good relations between China and the United States are of vital importance to peace and stability in East Asia and the Pacific, and at the global level as well, and would serve the national interests of both countries. Relations between the two countries in the 1950s and 1960s, however, were characterized by hostility to, and isolation from, each other. China and the United States began to move toward a rapprochement in late 1969, and, despite continuing differences over Taiwan and other issues, the two nations managed to maintain a steady and improving relationship for the next twenty years—until the spring of 1989. If there had not been the June 1989 events in Beijing, the Sino-American relationship, as expected by a majority of the two peoples and their leaders, might have entered a new decade of consultation and cooperation. However, the intense strains resulting from the Tiananmen Square events have brought U.S.-Chinese relations to their lowest point since 1972.

The American public and the U.S. Congress reacted swiftly and angrily to the events in Beijing. The Bush Administration immediately announced that it had imposed sanctions against China, including suspension of arms sales to and military exchanges with China. Two weeks later, on June 20, the White House announced further action, suspending high-level official contacts between the two governments.

In China, newspaper editorials and articles strongly criticized foreign interference in China's internal affairs, especially by the United States. China's formal official reaction, however, was more moderate. For instance, at a June 22 press conference, the spokeswoman of the Foreign Ministry, besides protesting interference by the United States and other Western countries in China's internal affairs, advised foreigners to observe recent events in China in a calm and cautious manner before drawing conclusions. The Chinese government never took any major retaliatory measures against the United States.

Instead, the Chinese Communist Party (CCP) and government made public a number of official statements and speeches by leaders including Deng Xiaoping's June 9 speech and his remarks on the development of the Four Cardinal Principles (keeping to the socialist road, upholding the people's democratic dictatorship, leadership by the Communist Party, and adherence to Mao Zedong thought) during the last ten years. These statements were published primarily to show that China's reform and open policy remains unchanged, to explain to foreigners the real situation in China, and also to express China's willingness to strengthen Sino-American relations on the basis of the Five Principles of Peaceful Coexistence.

Following his initial strong actions, President Bush refused to impose further sanctions against China. In an address on regional cooperation on June 26, 1989, Secretary of State James Baker stressed that human rights could not be the only factor in U.S. foreign policy decision-making. He warned that "The hasty dismantling of a constructive U.S.-Chinese relationship built up so carefully over two decades would serve neither our interests nor those of the Chinese people." An important step was taken by the Bush Administration when it sent National Security Adviser Brent Scowcroft and Deputy Secretary of State Lawrence Eagleburger as special envoys to Beijing on December 9. Then, from early 1990 on, various steps were taken in return on the Chinese side, including the lifting of martial law first in Beijing on January 1 and later in Tibet on May 1; the release of 573 detainees who had been held since June 4, 1989; and finally, the decision to permit Fang Lizhi to leave the U.S. Embassy in Beijing and go abroad on June 25, 1990.

These actions by the two governments and the signals sent to each other during the past year show clearly that there has been some improvement in the U.S.-Chinese relationship, though uncertainty about its future remains. It is difficult to predict the future of Sino-U.S. relations, but a cautious assessment suggests that this relationship, within the next two or three years, will neither deteriorate further nor improve rapidly. It is likely to remain largely unchanged.

The Sino-American relationship is too important to be placed in jeopardy, as the events of the past forty years have demonstrated. The first twenty years of animosity and isolation contributed to two wars in Asia which deeply involved the United States and China and cost them both dearly. The friendly relations enjoyed by both parties throughout the second twenty years, however, benefited them a great deal, not only strategically but also economically. The United States is no longer facing challenges on two fronts, and China is now enjoying a comparatively peaceful environment in which its people can concentrate their efforts on modernization. Although China is an underdeveloped country, its economy is growing and its economic influence will inevitably increase. China's healthy, growing economy with its population of 1.1 billion people is a stable factor in East Asia and the Pacific.

Differences in ideology and value systems continue to create significant barriers to improved relations between China and the United States. Its position as a superpower has often caused the United States to ignore the feelings and interests of other countries while attempting to impose its own system and values. For instance, the United States interfered with China's domestic politics on the issues of Tibet and family planning in the name of "human rights," thus injecting unpleasant factors into its bilateral relations with China and hurting the feelings of the Chinese people. Such action runs counter to Chinese interests as well as long-term U.S. interests, and the Chinese people find it very difficult to understand why the Americans engage in such open interference in other countries' internal affairs.

China's reform policies, begun at the end of 1978, have already achieved considerable progress in the economy and society, including the human rights sector. Since then and even in 1990, the Chinese people can openly discuss such issues as civil rights and freedom, subjects that were taboo during the Cultural Revolution. Most Chinese intellectuals who lived through both periods would agree that progress in this area has been remarkable.

Former President Richard Nixon once said that countries with different cultural backgrounds and at different stages of development need different systems. The United States should not use its own form of democracy to judge the governments of other countries. China and the United States have different political systems; each has its own national interests and is in a different stage of economic development. A system of democracy and human rights can only be attained when progress is made in a country's economy and society. Both China and the United States should focus their efforts on areas where their national interests are compatible rather than enlarging the gap between them through differences in ideology. In this way, stable bilateral relations can be nurtured over the long run.

The Taiwan problem has been the other key issue standing in the way of Sino-American normalization from the very beginning. Up until recently, the United States and China have had common concerns about Soviet expansionism in East Asia and elsewhere in the world, and this had tended to make the Taiwan problem a secondary issue. But this does not mean that the Taiwan obstacle has disappeared. The United States should not mistake China's patient policy toward Taiwan as abandonment of principle and of its ultimate goal of reunification.

In the 1972 Shanghai Joint Communique, the United States acknowledged that "there is but one China and Taiwan is a part of China; and in the Joint Communique of December 15, 1978, which announced that the two countries were establishing diplomatic relations with each other, the United States recognized the People's Republic of China as the "sole legal government of China." At the same time, the United States accepted the three conditions for normalization set by China: terminating diplomatic relations with Taiwan, abrogating the U.S.-Taiwan Mutual Defense Treaty, and withdrawing all remaining U.S. military personnel from Taiwan. But the question of continuing U.S. arms sales to Taiwan was put aside. On top of that, the U.S. Congress passed the Taiwan Relations Act soon after Sino-U.S. diplomatic relations were established. This was a major step backward in the U.S. position on Taiwan and indicates that the United States has never abandoned its policy of "one China, one Taiwan" or "two Chinas."

Although the United States repeatedly stated, over a period of time, that it would not interfere in China's internal politics, most Chinese assert the U.S. government has not only interfered but has legalized such interference in the form of the Taiwan Relations Act. As long as this legislation remains in effect, U.S. interference in China's domestic affairs cannot be considered over.

It should be made clear to all concerned that China will never allow Taiwan to be independent. If an effort is ever made to treat Taiwan as an independent state, the result would seriously harm both Sino-U.S. relations and the prospects for peace and stability in the Asian-Pacific region.

Currently, the new Chinese leadership is trying to strike a balance between the four cardinal principles on the one hand, and the reform and open policy on the other. It stresses that China must adhere unswervingly to the four cardinal principles, as the foundation of the country, and implement steadfastly the policy of reform and opening to the outside world, as the means for leading the country to strength and prosperity. However, if the United States continues to overemphasize the ideological differences between itself and China, China will react strongly and tighten "ideology control" severely and, in the worst possible scenario, close its door and abandon the policy of reform and opening to the rest of the world.

Some Americans have suggested that a number of signals must be given by China to regain American confidence. At this point, what is really needed is for the leaders of both governments to demonstrate enough courage and skill to break through the present stalemate in Sino-U.S. relations, just as Chairman Mao Zedong and President Richard M. Nixon did during a much more difficult time than we face today.

An American Perspective on Sino-U.S. Relations

The Tiananmen Square massacre set back, at least temporarily, the efforts of many years to build a stable relationship between China and the United States. For a generation after the accession to power of the Chinese communist government in 1949, the United States and China had been sometimes bitter opponents. It took a decade after 1969 for Beijing and Washington to move toward the establishment of full diplomatic relations. For the United States, China became an increasingly important part of the emerging multipolar world that was envisaged by the Nixon Administration, and a member of the proto-coalition arrayed against Soviet hegemonism from the late 1970s well into the 1980s.

By 1989, however, important changes had altered the role of China in the present geostrategic setting. In the midst of the Tiananmen Square demonstrations, in May 1989, Mikhail Gorbachev visited Beijing symbolizing the transformation of Sino-Soviet relations from hostility to accommodation toward normalization. Moscow had taken substantial political strides to meet China's preconditions for diplomatic normalization, including Soviet military withdrawal from Afghanistan, the removal of Vietnamese forces from Cambodia, and the dismantling of Soviet SS-20s targeted against China. In the Western media Gorbachev's visit to Beijing was all but overshadowed by images of Chinese students and workers gathered around the Goddess of

Democracy in Tiananmen Square that bore a close resemblance to the Statue of Liberty.

Had a Soviet leader visited Beijing a decade earlier, such an event would have been justifiably interpreted as having profoundly unsettling implications for the Eurasian and Asian-Pacific geostrategic setting. In the changed circumstances of the late 1980s, however, China's geostrategic role, while by no means eliminated as a fundamental element in any Asian-Pacific balance, had become a less urgent consideration in American policy as the U.S. relationship with the Soviet Union entered a new phase with Moscow's mounting economic problems and Gorbachev's domestic challenges. Such was the setting in which the Sino-American relationship unfolded at the end of the 1980s and into the present decade, in which it became increasingly difficult, if no less necessary, for the United States to balance enduring geostrategic interests and justified concerns about human rights highlighted by the Tiananmen Square massacre.

In the aftermath of Tiananmen Square, the United States now has a more realistic understanding of the measures that the Beijing government is prepared to take in order to stifle dissent and to assure its own survival. By the same token, the Chinese leadership may have gained a greater insight into the limits of American willingness (or ability) to subordinate human rights to the needs of a geostrategic relationship. In the age of instantaneous images transmitted globally by television, the ability of any Chinese government to conceal repressive measures such as the Tiananmen Square massacre will continue to diminish. As such incidents are more widely seen by viewers on an international scale, it will become even more difficult for the United States to separate the geostrategic dimensions of its relationship with China from the Chinese leadership's treatment of dissidents.

Hence, the United States has an obvious interest in the evolution of China toward a more moderate, tolerant government committed to a freer press, a legal system based on protection of individual rights, and a market-oriented economy. In opposing such trends, China in the early 1990s stands at odds with the breathtaking transformation that has swept away communist regimes in Eastern Europe. The extent to which the present leadership can continue to resist these tides remains to be seen. Yet China is one of the world's great civilizations with a long and rich history that for centuries has stood against unwanted influences from the outside world. As such, China understandably will continue to resent and resist outside advice about how to manage its internal affairs. Moreover, its communist leadership, having witnessed the fate of its counterparts in Eastern Europe as well as Gorbachev's problems in the

Soviet Union, will not willingly embark on policies whose effect would be to undermine its very existence. Paradoxically, the changes that have pointed up the intractable contradictions of communist regimes elsewhere and have the potential to spill over into China itself will make the Chinese political elite even less willing than otherwise might have been the case to accept major reforms.

Whatever its views of the domestic politics of China, the United States will need, as illustrated by recent events in the Middle East, either to enlist China's cooperation or to forestall its opposition in regional conflicts in which both countries have interests. As a result, the United States will find it necessary to develop a more balanced relationship with China that somehow reconciles our international security needs with our values about acceptable domestic political practices.

China's Internal Dynamics in the 1990s: Political, Economic and Social Trends

by Jürgen Domes

Political scientists are not prophets, and on most occasions when they have presumed to fill that role, their predictions have turned out to be inaccurate. Lacking the assistance of "a crystal ball," it is impossible to predict conclusively how the internal political situation in the People's Republic of China (PRC) will develop during the next decade. Nevertheless, this paper will offer several plausible alternative projections, in the form of scenarios—each of which has its own level of probability. First, it is necessary to describe China's domestic condition at the point of departure—the summer of 1989. Next, we will examine the major forces that are presumed to be critical in shaping future developments. Then, we will set forth alternative projections regarding China's future, and, finally, advance some brief and tentative thoughts regarding possible consequences for Western, and especially American, policymaking.

The PRC in 1989

From April 17 through June 3, 1989, first tens of thousands and ultimately millions of Chinese—initially, mainly university students, but increasingly, people from all walks of life among the urban population—held demonstrations in Beijing and at least sixteen other Chinese cities, demanding human rights, freedom, and democracy. From May 4 through June 3, demonstrators occupied the very center of China's capital, Tiananmen Square, established their own autonomous organizations and unions, policed major parts of Beijing, and began to develop spontaneously their own administrative networks.

In the early morning hours of June 4, units of the armed forces—the People's Liberation Army (PLA)—moved in with tanks, armored personnel carriers, and a variety of other weapons, suffocating the movement in a sudden massacre in which between 2,500 and 8,000 citizens were killed in Beijing alone, most of whom were unarmed.

Starting on June 6, the Chinese Communist Party (CCP) launched a nationwide campaign of Stalinist terror, arresting some 20,000 people, and executing at least 29 participants in the pro-democracy movement during the month of June alone.

These events have dramatically changed the domestic political scene in the PRC. After the Spring Crisis of 1989, the optimistic projections about China's future that had been advanced by a host of politicians, businessmen, and journalists in almost all Western countries, and by a large group of China specialists in the West, could no longer be sustained. They had contended that the policies of economic reform and of opening to the outside world, enacted by the ruling elite since 1978-1979, had become "irreversible," and that the country appeared to be leaning toward domestic political openness if not democracy. Hence, to these euphoric and apologetic observers, the Spring Crisis came unexpectedly. Yet not all China specialists in the West, not even all those in the United States, had taken such optimistic views. Indeed, for those who had continued to observe developments in the PRC in a detached, analytical manner, the crisis did not come as a surprise. It was unfolding, rather, over the previous four or more years, and should not have startled anyone who had stayed in close touch with the China scene.

The policies of economic reform had, in the ten years from early 1979 to late 1988, resulted in remarkable success. The average real GNP growth rate for these ten years stood at 8.33 percent annually. From 1979 through 1985 alone, grain production had increased from 304.75 to 378.98 million tons, a growth of 24.4 percent overall, and in terms of per capita grain production, an increase of 13.8 percent. In 1987, grain production rose further to 402.41 million tons, amounting to an overall increase of 32 percent since 1979, and raising per capita production by 17.2 percent.[1] Growth rates in industry, particularly for light and consumer goods, were even more impressive. The PRC's share in world trade more than doubled from 0.8 percent in 1978 to 1.7 percent in 1988. Personal income rose significantly, and the gap between rural and urban income narrowed from a ratio of 1:3.14 in 1978 to 1:1.89 in 1985.[2]

In 1985, however, the first signs that the country was moving into an economic crisis could be detected. This crisis fully manifested itself during 1988, affecting the entire society. For one thing, the economy

---

[1]Hsueh Mu-ch'iao, editor, *Zhongguo jingji nian-jian 1982 (Almanac of China's Economy, 1982)* (Beijing: Economic Management Publishing Corporation, 1982), parts 8, 5, and 16 f; *Renmin Ribao (People's Daily)*, Beijing (hereafter cited as *RMRB*), February 28, 1986, February 24, 1988.

[2]Ibid.

started to overheat, with the real GNP growth rate rising to 11.2 percent in 1988. This growth, however, was uneven. While industrial production showed a real growth of 17.7 percent from 1987 to 1988, grain production fell 2.1 percent from 402.41 million tons in 1987 to 394.01 million tons in 1988, which meant a decline of 3.5 percent in per capita grain production.[3] Since the mid-1980s, income differentials have progressively widened. By the end of 1988, the gap between rural and urban income had widened to 1:2.05.[4] Overall, the Gini coefficient for the PRC had risen from between 0.38 and 0.43 in 1978 to between 0.44 and 0.47 in 1987.[5]

Moreover, inflation became a serious problem in 1988. The official inflation rates had been 8.8 percent in 1985, 6 in 1986, 7.9 in 1987, and 18.5 in 1988.[6] In fact, the real inflation rate in 1988 was probably between 30 and 35 percent; by May 1989 the official figure was up to 27 percent.[7] The dramatic price increases primarily affected industrial workers, teaching personnel at all levels of education, and a large portion of the intelligentsia. According to official data, 34.9 percent of all urban households suffered a decrease in real income during 1988.[8]

Theoretically, this surge in inflation also affected the cadres in the party and in the state administrative machine, but many of them have always been able to supplement their income by taking bribes and accepting gifts. This practice became more widespread throughout the 1980s, until by early 1987, all levels of the party organization and state administration in the PRC were involved in bribery, embezzlement, and other illicit ways of increasing personal wealth. These practices permeate the whole system to such a degree that by now the PRC is undoubtedly the most corrupt country in all of East and Southeast Asia. When the CCP media revealed that more than 45,700 cases of corruption involving 8,777 cadres had been investigated and tried by the courts during 1988,[9] that disclosure clearly was only "the tip of the iceberg."

---

[3]Computed by the author from data published in *RMRB*, March 1, 1989.

[4]Ibid.

[5]For 1978, see William Parish, "Egalitarianism in Chinese Society," *Problems of Communism*, Vol. 30, No. 1, January/February 1981, p. 41; for 1987, calculations by the author on the basis of more than 1,400 pieces of data from various official PRC media sources. The Gini coefficient is an indicator for the distribution of the national income of a given country over five different income groups. The closer it is to zero, the more equal the distribution; the closer it is to one, the more unequal the distribution.

[6]*RMRB*, March 1, 1986; February 21, 1987; February 24, 1988; and March 1, 1989.

[7]*RMRB*, May 9, 1986.

[8]*RMRB*, March 1, 1989.

[9]*RMRB* (overseas edition), March 30, 1989.

These signs of increasing economic and social decay were aggravated by the fact that, from the early- to the mid-1980s, the Marxist-Leninist doctrine had progressively lost its motivating force for a growing portion of the Chinese populace. The peasants had benefited most from the core element of the economic reform policies that had been enacted by Deng Xiaoping and his associates since 1979—the de-collectivization of agricultural production within the framework of continued collective ownership of the arable land. Those who had profited from the new rural policies continued their support for the ruling elite, primarily because it was in their best interests to do so and under the condition that these policies would not be changed—a prevailing concern among many peasants. Yet such support was not expressed through political activity, and was not based on a belief in the doctrines of the CCP; rather, the peasants sought to make optimal use of all opportunities to improve their individual living conditions.

Engineers, foremen, and the better paid of the urban workers profited, too, from the policies of economic reform until 1987. Yet, for them, the impact of inflation gradually eroded their trust in the party and its doctrine. This disillusionment also set in for the workers in the middle and lower wage brackets. Having developed very high expectations during the initial stages of economic reform, many of them became increasingly disappointed. Hence, this group ceased to believe in the ideology of Marxism-Leninism and started to display a rising propensity toward dissent. The same holds true for the urban poor, except that they must struggle daily just to secure the basic necessities for survival and thus have neither the time nor the energy for dissent.

The new private entrepreneurs in the PRC—"self-employed workers" and owners of "individual enterprises"—are the only group, besides the upper and middle income groups among the peasantry, that has profited greatly from the policies of the reform-oriented revisionists within the leadership. They were afraid, however, that a return to stricter socialist doctrines could threaten their survival by inhibiting their ability to make money. Hence, while supporting the policies of economic reform, they were skeptical about the Marxist-Leninist doctrine. Moreover, members of these groups were increasingly pressured to offer bribes to certain party activists, and often, if these bribes were considered unsatisfactory, their lives were made difficult. Many small entrepreneurs suffered from high rents which were levied if they operated state-owned "means of production"—for example, taxicabs or trucks—on a contractual basis.

Yet the most negative attitudes toward party doctrine were to be found among the young people, particularly college and university students. The majority of urban youths, and an increasing number of young people in the more affluent village areas as well, cared mainly about their careers and about enjoying life to the fullest extent that their still very limited means allowed. Since the early 1980s, many young people have adopted an attitude of total cynicism toward the doctrine of Marxism-Leninism, and thus a spiritual and moral crisis has pervaded the younger generation, particularly in the cities and among the students.[10] The CCP media began reporting in 1980 that many young people believe "socialism cannot match capitalism."[11] The youths asked: "Can socialism really save China?...The fatherland is so backward, how can one love it?"[12] Since 1984, the media have continued to admit that the youth of the PRC was in the midst of a "crisis of three faiths," that it had—and has—no faith in the party, no faith in socialism, and no faith in the fatherland. This situation was also reflected by the fact that young people were increasingly hesitant to become members of the CCP: In 1985 only 2.25 percent of those aged eighteen to thirty were party members, compared to about 7.5 percent of the whole adult population who claimed membership,[13] and this figure has not changed significantly during the past five years.

Thus, the Marxist-Leninist ideology in the PRC was facing a severe crisis by the second half of the 1980s. It had become stale and had lost its credibility to such an extent that, apart from about 800 persons in the ruling elite, and an uncertain number of orthodox stalwarts among the party cadres and members, by 1988 very few in the PRC still subscribed to the Marxist-Leninist doctrine. Ideological apathy, cynicism, and increasingly open opposition to party doctrine had become a widespread trend.

In the summer of 1988 the ruling elite, faced with a major economic crisis and the erosion of the legitimating ideology, had to decide how to solve these crises—by introducing further and even more audacious economic reforms, or by freezing these reforms at the current level. Consensus on these issues among the leadership dissipated during the ensuing debate. In the second half of July 1988, the Politburo and the Standing Committee of the Central Advisory Commission of the CCP held a "work conference." The reform-oriented revisionists, led by the CCP Central Committee's Secretary General,[14] Zhao Ziyang, confronted the orthodox

---

[10]Cf. Thomas P. Gold, "China's Youth: Problems and Programs," in Chang Ching-yü, editor, *The Emerging Teng System: Orientation, Policies, and Implications* (Taipei: Institute of International Relations, 1983), part IV-2, pp. 1-24.

[11]Sichuan People's Broadcasting Station (hereafter cited as PBS), March 2, 1980.

[12]*RMRB*, March 19, 1981.

[13]*RMRB*, May 16, 1985.

[14]It should be pointed out that the Secretary General of the CCP Central Committee is not

group, led by Prime Minister Li Peng, First Vice-Premier Yao Yilin, and the increasingly influential Chairman of the Central Advisory Commission, Chen Yun. To counter the economic crisis, Zhao proposed to decontrol almost all prices and to limit further the powers of the central planning organs. His proposal, however, was rejected by the majority at the conference, and Chen Yun moved to dismiss Zhao from his position as Secretary General. This motion was not put to a vote and the conference adjourned until mid-August. When it reconvened, Chen and Deng Xiaoping had worked out a compromise: The motion to dismiss Zhao was withdrawn, but it was decided that the special responsibilities within the Politburo's Standing Committee should be re-assigned: Zhao had to cede the responsibility for economic policies to Li Peng and Yao Yilin.[15]

The third plenum of the Thirteenth CCP Central Committee (CCP/CC), which convened in Beijing from September 29 through October 1, approved a draft report prepared by Li and Yao, which effectively put the brakes on the policies of economic reform. Under the slogan, "Deepen the reforms, improve the economic environment, and restore economic order!," the plenum called for drastic cuts in investments, particularly in construction projects, and for a strengthening of the centralized planning element.[16] A few days later, the PRC government instituted fixed prices or price-ceilings for 326 groups of products, the prices of which had been decontrolled since early 1985.

Developments during the winter of 1988-1989 rendered it difficult to implement these new economic policies. Officials in many provinces were hesitant to carry out these policies and some even flatly refused to do so; on the local level, also, obedience to central directives declined significantly. Thus, the political system had begun to disintegrate—a condition that was further aggravated by rising social unrest and an escalation of the intra-elite conflict over power and policies between the orthodox and the revisionist groups within the leadership, which split off into quarreling factions.

---

in a position that is comparable to, e.g., the General Secretary of the CPSU. He is not the "party leader," but the person in charge of the administrative work of the civilian party machine. The CCP is collectively led by the Standing Committee of the Politburo, of which, to date, the Secretary General is one among six members.

[15]See the reports of "Lo Ping" in *Cheng-ming* (Debate), Hong Kong, No. 130, August 1988, pp. 6-10; and No. 131, September 1988, pp. 6-11. Cf. James F. Sterba, "Long March: How the Twisting Path of China's Reform Led to Guns of Tiananmen," *Wall Street Journal*, June 16, 1989.

[16]"Communique of the Third Plenum of the Thirteenth CCP/CC," October 1, 1988; *RMRB*, October 2, 1988.

Rising inflation compounded social unrest. Wage raises, bonus increases, and large handouts of inflation relief payments could not halt the slide in real income experienced by all urban public employees, including workers at state-owned enterprises—comprising in 1988, 88 percent of urban labor[17]—scientists, university instructors, school teachers, journalists, the majority of medical personnel, many artists and writers, and the cadres of the party and the state administrative machine. Only the latter groups were able to counter their loss of real income by taking bribes and embezzling. Thus, by 1988 the CCP ruling elite had lost almost all of its urban support.

Hence, the reasons for the Spring Crisis of 1989 become clear: a strong wave of urban discontent with elite policy coinciding with a major intra-elite conflict over power and policies.

The immediate result of the crisis itself was the violent suppression of the Democracy Movement. The orthodox faction, strengthened by the shift of Deng Xiaoping toward support of its policies, won the intra-elite conflict. Repressive measures by the PRC confirm the fact that, for the time being, it has moved in the direction of a neo-Stalinist bureaucratic socialism.

This does not mean, however, that the CCP ruling elite has won more than a Pyrrhic victory. Although this elite succeeded, once again, in stifling a strong opposition movement, the massacres in Beijing, Chengdu, Sian, Changsha, and probably other cities, and the subsequent campaign of terror have destroyed the last vestiges of legitimacy which the CCP might still have commanded before June 4, 1989. Since the first week of June, popular resistance has assumed different dimensions from those of the Democracy Movement in April and May. The fact that, six weeks after the Beijing massacre, fourteen of the twenty-one most wanted student leaders of the movement were still free, and that at least four had escaped from the country, clearly indicated a lack of support for the leaders of the PRC. Even many CCP members seem reluctant to follow the central leadership. Deng Xiaoping clearly suggested this in a speech given to the officers of the Beijing intervention forces on June 9 by stating that it would take "a long time of hard work [to convince] Party members that the action [of June 4] was necessary."[18] Meanwhile, two trains had been bombed; in Beijing, many shop owners refused to serve PLA soldiers;[19] and in mid-July, the Beijing office of Japan Airlines received a letter from an underground

---

[17]RMRB, March 1, 1989.

[18]RMRB, June 27, 1989.

[19]Jiefangjun Bao (*Liberation Army Daily*), Beijing, July 12, 1989.

organization threatening to kill Japanese businessmen who continued to deal with the CCP ruling elite.[20]   These were only scattered incidents, but one may well argue that the Spring Crisis of 1989 could one day mark the beginning of the end of communist rule in China.

Forces in PRC Politics

A review of the forces that can be expected to shape political developments in the PRC during the 1990s cannot, therefore, be limited to the ruling elite, the CCP, and the PLA. It also has to take into account the opposition, and Chinese society as a whole.   In the following sections, I will examine the current situation and forecast possible trends for all of these elements.

The Ruling Elite and the Party

At an enlarged meeting of the Politburo which took place from June 19 to 21, 1989, the intra-elite conflict between the orthodox and the revisionist factions was finally resolved in favor of the former, and this victory by the orthodox faction was ratified at the fourth plenum of the Thirteenth CCP/CC, which convened in Beijing on June 23 and 24.[21]   The purge, however, was confined to four leaders.   Zhao Ziyang and Hu Qili were dismissed from the Standing Committee of the Politburo, the Politburo, and the Secretariat, and Rui Xingwen and Yan Minfu from the Secretariat.   Since then, the inner leadership core—the Standing Committee of the Politburo—has consisted of five orthodox politicians: the new Secretary General of the CCP/CC, Jiang Zemin (62 years of age); Prime Minister Li Peng (61); Qiao Shi(65), leader of the security apparatus; First Vice Premier Yao Yilin (72); and Song Ping (72), the second newly appointed member of this body and Director of the CCP/CC's Organization Department.   Only the sixth member of this group, the former Mayor of Tianjin, Li Ruihuan (55), can be described as a reformist-oriented revisionist. Currently, the whole Politburo has only fourteen members and one alternate, nine of whom can be considered orthodox[22] and only four revisionist.[23]   The political preferences of one member and of the alternate remain unclear.[24]   This, however, does not

[20]*San Francisco Examiner*, July 19, 1989.

[21]*RMRB*, June 25, 1989.

[22]Jiang Zemin, Li Peng, Qiao Shi, Yao Yilin, Song Ping, General Yang Shangkun (82), Li Ximing (63), Li Tieying (53), and Wu Xueqian (68).

[23]Li Ruihuan, Wan Li (73), Tian Jiyun (60), and General Qin Jiwei (75).

[24]Yang Rudai (63) and the alternate member Ding Guangen(60).

8

paint an accurate picture of the factional lineup within the ruling elite. Since the Spring Crisis of 1989, the political influence of a number of veteran revolutionaries has greatly increased. Here, besides Deng Xiaoping (85) and Chen Yun (84), the two most influential leaders in the PRC, we must mention Vice President General Wang Zhen (81), Song Renqiong (80), and the traditional Stalinists, Li Xiannian (84) and Bo Yibo (80). Except for Deng, who supported the economic reform policies, though not the political ones, they all have consistently taken orthodox positions, and it must therefore be expected that they will influence PRC politics in the direction of strong central planning and strict discipline under the doctrine of Marxism-Leninism.

Yet time will take its toll on these leaders. It can be expected that, by the early- to mid-1990s, all or at least most of the veterans will be gone from the political scene. If there is no further major intra-elite conflict which brings about significant changes in leadership personnel—a proposition that is by no means certain—this would leave the current Politburo members at the helm of the party by the early- to mid-1990s. They have now, if one includes the alternate, an average age of 65.7 years. No clear age distinctions among the adherents of the two political tendencies—orthodox and revisionist—are apparent. The nine orthodox Politburo members have now an average age of 66.4 years, the four revisionists of 65.8 years. Among the five youngest members (including the alternate) there are two orthodox, two revisionists, and one whose position is unclear. This means that no radical policy changes can be expected to occur as a result of the age factor. Moreover, a review of the fifteen youngest members of the CCP/CC, whose current positions make it likely that they may advance to the Politburo in the foreseeable future, provides no additional clues: Six or seven of them must be considered orthodox, five or six revisionist, and the positions of three remain unclear.

One observation, however, can be made with certainty: The events of May and June 1989 have left the party in a very difficult political situation, as far as internal party coherence and discipline are concerned. On May 24, when the provincial party leadership groups hastened to declare their support for the state of emergency and, hence, their loyalty to the current leadership, six out of thirty provinces were conspicuously missing from the fold—among them, the economically strong provinces of Guangdong and Liaoning.[25] This may be a portent of future dissension in the PRC.

---

[25]Zhejiang, Jiangxi, Guangxi Zhuang, Guangdong, Guizhou and Liaoning. See *RMRB*, May 24, 1989.

Critically important for the development of the party's role in China's future political dynamics is the extent of its members' commitment to the Marxist-Leninist doctrine. Central to this doctrine is the Leninist concept of leadership by the Communist Party. The ruling elite of about 800 CCP politicians and at least the majority of the approximately 80,000 "leading cadres" seem to be fully pledged to the doctrine, and for good reasons: It guarantees their claim to rule, enables them to impede the development of competing elites and to suppress dissent, and it ensures their manifold privileges.

The importance of the doctrine to the 47 million members of the Communist Party is more difficult to assess. The approximately 18 to 19 million members, who, as cadres at all levels, have access to privileges and can supplement their incomes by taking kickbacks, are surely committed to the core of the doctrine. Nevertheless, the question remains whether ideology continues to be a major motivating force. The simple party members—the almost 30 million without positions of even local leadership—seem to regard the party mainly as a career channel, an avenue of upward mobility. There may be a number of truly believing orthodox stalwarts among them, but if there are any, they have remained relatively quiet in the last five years, particularly during the Spring Crisis of 1989. When a foreign observer, traveling in the PRC or meeting CCP members abroad, asks what Marxism-Leninism means, very often he gets nebulous replies such as "I do not really know," or "It is the doctrine of the Party, but it is not very familiar to me," or, at best, "It means to love our fatherland."[26]

In summary: Within the CCP, intra-elite conflicts will very likely continue during the next decade. Dedication to the cause of Marxism-Leninism is not very widespread among its members, and the events that took place during the spring of 1989 have further weakened the morale of the party, leaving it a still important, but significantly weakened force in PRC politics.

The Military

It was the PLA that suppressed the Democracy Movement in Beijing and other cities in the massacre of June 4, 1989. In the past, the PLA played the decisive role in PRC crises during the Cultural Revolution in 1967 and the summer of 1968, and during the conflict over the succession to Mao Zedong when it engineered the military coup d'etat of October 6, 1976. It can be assumed that the PLA will intervene again in future crises. Yet one may well question whether the military will continue to

---

[26]Based on the personal experiences of the author.

support the ruling elite in such periods of crisis. In late May and early June 1989, there was some evidence that factions within the PLA were opposed to the crackdown on the Democracy Movement. On May 22, seven retired, prestigious army generals warned in a letter to the party center against employing the PLA to enforce the state of emergency declared on May 20.[27] Although this move was countered by the Chief of the General Staff, the directors of the PLA General Political and General Rear Services Departments, and six out of seven Military Area Commanders, who wrote an open letter declaring their full support for the emergency order,[28] difficulties did arise within the military in the context of the massacre. Such difficulties did not at the time pose a grave danger to the ruling elite, although there was scattered insubordination. In the province of Jilin, some units mutinied together with a number of their officers,[29] and in Beijing, some soldiers and officers took off their uniforms, changed to civilian clothes, and disappeared during the early morning hours of June 4.[30]

The generational change in the military command positions, which took place between 1985 and 1987, replaced the politically active veterans of the "Long March" and the civil war, who had a clear record of political involvement, with more professional military leaders. The current age range of the active top leadership of the PLA is 48 to 70, the average age is about 61 years, and the overwhelming majority are between 58 and 68 years of age. This means that, apart from the oldest and the youngest in the group, most were between 19 and 29 when the PRC entered the Korean War. Thus, the generation of PLA officers who were platoon leaders to company commanders during the Korean War is now in active command. This generation is much more thoroughly educated in military techniques than their predecessors, and they have displayed little political activity thus far. Hence, it is impossible to predict their future political attitudes. It can be proposed with reasonable confidence that the PLA will continue to press for an augmented military budget, which has suffered drastic cuts over the last decade, and that it may make such an increase a condition for its continuing support of the ruling elite. This, in turn, will put additional strains on an already heavily burdened state budget.

Support by generals and the officer corps, including the political

---

[27]Text of this letter in excerpts in *Chung-kuo shih-pao* (*China Times*), T'aipei (hereafter cited as *CKSP*), May 23, 1989.

[28]*RMRB*, May 24, 1989.

[29]Jilin *PBS*, June 11 and 13, 1989.

[30]Information provided to the author by citizens of the PRC in the United States, June and July 1989.

commissars, however, does not necessarily translate into support by the rank-and-file, or, in particular, by the draftees, who comprise slightly more than half of all PLA soldiers. Even before the Spring Crisis, a steep decline in the PLA's prestige presented material and psychological difficulties for rank-and-file professional soldiers and draftees. Peasant families of draftees and of professional soldiers were missing one working person, and, hence, in many areas of the PRC, they received less arable land to till. In addition, while peasant girls were eager to marry soldiers in earlier times, they started shunning them after 1980-1981: The low salaries of the soldiers made them less attractive "catches" than during the 1960s and 1970s when members of the PLA enjoyed important privileges, particularly in the distribution of consumer goods, which are now rather commonplace. After the Beijing massacre of June 4, the PLA's prestige fell off drastically. Students were calling it the "People's Liquidation Army" in English or *Chung-kuo sha-min chieh-fang-chün* in Chinese, which can be translated as "Chinese People's Killers Liberation Army."[31] Hence, the PLA is a military force under severe psychological stress, and it is not a foregone conclusion that it will still be a loyal and readily available tool of the ruling elite when the next major political crisis erupts. Both party and army, thus, appear to be somewhat unreliable and unstable institutions. Whatever their responses to elite policies may be during the next decade, they are definitely no longer the only viable forces shaping politics in the PRC. Since the events of May and June 1989, opposition groups have become part of any political equation.

The Opposition

Although the PRC has a long history of dissent, opposition against the Marxist-Leninist single-party dictatorship was, for over three decades, very poorly organized at best. Among the noteworthy cases of dissension are the "hundred flowers campaign" that took place in the spring of 1957, the wave of criticism directed at Mao Zedong by party intellectuals in 1960-1961, the activities of radical "Red Guard" groups in Hunan, Zhejiang, and Guangdong in 1967-1968, the anti-Maoist demonstrations in April 1976, and the Democracy and Human Rights Movement in 1978-1979.

Already in the early 1970s, the nuclei of opposition had begun to form in some cities, but it was only in the early 1980s that they started to develop into a still rather weak network. Gradually, a number of small urban circles evolved, which combined the remnants of Red Guard

---

[31]Ibid.

12

organizations of the late 1960s with those forces of the Democracy and Human Rights Movement of 1978-1979 that went underground when this movement was suppressed in 1979-1980. These circles actively opposed the policies of the ruling elite with a general platform calling for freedom of speech, information, assembly, and association as well as for competitive elections; they sought to introduce elements of a participatory political culture into China's official political system.

These circles were soon joined by students who had returned from advanced studies in Western countries; after the suppression of the Student Democracy Movement of November-December 1986, a large number of students from universities, colleges, and senior high schools within the PRC joined as well. Since early 1987, workers, particularly younger ones, also began to link up with these circles. Yet they had no national organization and remained uncoordinated; until the spring of 1989, it appeared that these circles still had a long time to go until they could become a viable political force. Thus, it seemed safe to assume that the CCP, being the only nationally organized political force, would continue its rule unchallenged, if only through default by its active opponents.

During the months of April and May 1989, however, the rudimentary, localized beginnings of an organized opposition were engulfed by the vehemence of the Democracy Movement. In its context, the opposition started to organize itself on a large scale. First in Beijing, and soon in a number of other cities, "autonomous federations" and "autonomous unions"—consciously following the model of the Polish Solidarity movement—were established, composed of students, workers, intellectuals, and even government officials and journalists working in the official media. These organizations established informal interregional contacts, and it appeared that they were on the verge of forming a nationwide network, when the ruling elite started to suppress the movement. The days between the proclamation of martial law on May 20 and the massacre in Beijing on June 4, however, appear to have been used by the opposition groups to prepare for underground activities. Despite the official ban on the autonomous organizations, there are indications that these groups continue at least some of their activities, and that they are strengthening their contacts. At the same time, a number of anti-CCP organizations have been formed among the students as well as PRC exchange scholars living abroad, and they either openly defy the regime or work clandestinely against its policies.

Thus, in 1989 the opposition achieved greater organizational strength than it had before. Yet even more important forces, which will shape future political developments in the PRC, are increasingly evident in

Chinese society. In fact, it was these forces that made the democracy movement in the spring of 1989 more than just another abortive attempt to democratize China.

The Society

In the 1950s, some of the more simplistic hypotheses which emerged from the theory of totalitarianism suggested that, in the so-called totalitarian states, an extremely efficient elite imposed its will upon a totally silent populace. Careful observation of more than seven decades of Marxist-Leninist regimes, and of almost four decades of PRC history, however, requires one to take a more discriminating approach to the explanation of interactions between the elite and society in totalitarian single-party systems in general, and particularly in the PRC.

I suggest that the seizure of power by totalistic elites and the stability of political systems established and dominated by such elites depend upon their success in forging and sustaining social coalitions or in preventing the evolution of such coalitions directed against the elites. In any given society, each stratum of the populace develops specific hopes, expectations, and demands. Elites are only able to seize power if they manage to respond to these needs, and in order to stay in power, they must, at least occasionally, renew such responsiveness. The term "social coalition" is defined here as a loose alliance that accumulates the demands of different strata of society—demands that are usually, though not always, inherent rather than precisely enunciated.[32]

Before the price inflation and the ensuing disintegration of society in 1987-1988, the policies of the ruling elite were generally supported by a social coalition of leading cadres, a sizable group of mid-level cadres, the majority of the technological and scientific intelligentsia, engineers, the higher paid industrial workers, and the newly emerging private owners of small urban individual enterprises. Those peasants who profited from the decollectivization of agricultural production—which we may reasonably estimate at about two-thirds of the peasantry or approximately 47 to 48 percent of PRC citizens—tolerated the current ruling elite as long as it guaranteed the continuation of its rural policies.

During 1988 and up until the spring of 1989, one group after another left the social coalition which had, until then, supported the ruling elite. Thus, a rather formidable new social coalition has evolved, and displays an increasing propensity toward active opposition. It is now composed of

---

[32]For details, see my *The Government and Politics of the PRC: A Time of Transition* (Boulder, CO: Westview Press, 1985), pp. 57-60, 229-231.

almost the entire young intelligentsia in the humanities, the majority of the technological and scientific intelligentsia, the students, many apprentices and young workers, most of industrial labor, the majority of employees in commerce and services, artists, writers, many journalists, and most owners of small, individual enterprises. In other words, during the last one and a half years, almost the entire urban society of the PRC has emancipated itself from the party. The basic political contradiction today is no longer that between the ruling elite and small circles of poorly organized yet active oppositionists; instead, it is the contradiction between the ruling elite and the urban citizenry.

Indeed, the process of separation between the party and society reached an advanced stage during and after the Spring Crisis of 1989. Yet, the extent of the effect that these fundamental social developments have had on the 78 percent of the PRC's population who live in the countryside—particularly the 68 percent of the population who make their living by farming—still remains a question. Are they on the verge of a nationwide peasant rebellion? The answer is no. Despite more than three decades of political campaigns, mobilization attempts, passive and active resistance between 1950 and 1980-1981, the Chinese countryside is still divided into approximately four to six million virtually unintegrated societies with nearly pure parochial political cultures. These minuscule polities have time and again successfully resisted all attempts at integrating them into a nationwide culture, and so far they have shown no interest in a nationwide drive toward systemic change. Nor have the peasants shown any inclination to form an organization that could aggregate and articulate peasant interests on a supra-village level.

This does not mean, however, that the countryside will be immune to social unrest in the foreseeable future. To the contrary, social unrest may occur locally if the government is forced, due to lack of funds, to pay half of the 20 billion yuan necessary to buy contracted grain—a process that usually starts in mid-August—at low prices and with debit notes instead of cash.[33] Should this occur, the quest by the peasants for title deeds to the land they now till individually under contracts, which would mean a decollectivization of land ownership, will become very strong. Property rights to the land is one of the demands which periodically have been articulated in some areas by the peasantry. Another is the quest for the freedom of childbirth—the demand for a drastic revision, if not the abolition, of birth control policies enacted by the current ruling elite. It is conceivable that the peasants may confront the Marxist-Leninist rulers

---

[33]*Nongmin Ribao* (*Peasants' Daily*) and *China Daily*, both Beijing, quoted without date by Sterba, op. cit.

with these two demands in the not-too-distant future. If this occurs, the crisis of the PRC's political system, which has already become evident in the cities, will spread to the countryside as well.

Even if the Chinese countryside does not rebel within the next few years, the process of liberating urban society from the party has already brought about revolutionary change on the Chinese political scene. The impetus for change has been set into motion and has become a major political factor. The future perspectives for the political system have definitely assumed a new quality: They can no longer be projected solely in the context of CCP single-party rule.

Perspectives

For the next year or two, we cannot expect the PRC to return to "normalcy." Under the impact of increased repression, the Chinese people will try to circumvent the political system and the demands of the ruling elite to an even greater extent than they have during the last five years, and they will use bribery and the cadres' propensity for corruption to mellow the grip of the regime. To give one example: Less than four weeks after the Beijing massacre, the newly introduced special exit permits—which PRC citizens must now obtain prior to application for foreign visas—could be bought from corrupt cadres for 7,500 yuan a piece in Shanghai, and for US$2,000 or Hong-Kong $12,000 in Canton, where the national currency is obviously no longer held in any confidence.[34] Moreover, the Chinese people will increasingly move away from the socialist economic system toward an ever expanding parallel or second economy of moonlighting, black marketeering, illegal exchange of foreign currency, underground banking, and underground production. This trend is bound to weaken the structures of social control, although those of political control may be strengthened for the immediate future. This means that societal policies in general will be more and more difficult to implement. In particular, the birth-control and family-planning policies, which have shown major deficiencies since 1986, and were verging on failure in 1988, are likely to collapse altogether, and the education and public health systems will continue to deteriorate.

Even without taking into account the perspectives for the political system, the social and economic trends which can be expected for the next decade do not leave much room for optimism from the ruling elite's point of view.

---

[34]See footnote 30 for sources.

In April 1989, the official population figure surpassed 1.1 billion. This figure, however, does not include the roughly 25 to 35 million so-called "black babies," those children born in defiance of the ruling elite's family-planning laws and hidden from the authorities.[35] Even if the official population growth rate as of 1988 remains constant at 1.43 percent until the mid-1990s, and then drops to 1.3 and further to 1.2 percent, the PRC would have between 1.29 and 1.3 billion inhabitants by the year 2000, or 100 million more than originally planned. In reality, this figure could even grow to 1.35 or 1.4 billion. Population growth puts severe strains on economic development. During the early 1980s, the goal of the ruling elite was to achieve a per capita GNP of US$800 at a constant 1985 value by the year 2000. This goal appeared realistic, but in order to reach it, real per capita GNP growth must remain constant at 7 percent right through 2000. If it should attain 8 percent—a rather unlikely long-term projection over ten years—the per capita GNP would reach US$895. At 6 percent real growth annually, it would only reach US$757 by 2000, and at 5 percent, US$670. Indeed, even if an annual per capita growth rate of 7 percent could be sustained, this would bring the PRC only to the level which South Yemen and Nicaragua had reached in 1985. This means that the PRC will remain an underdeveloped country with very limited prospects for accelerated modernization through and beyond the end of the 20th century. Moreover, it is unlikely that, within the next few years, the ruling elite, ridden with political and social problems, will be able to solve the three major economic problems with which the PRC is beset: inflation, energy shortfalls, and shortages of raw and semi-processed materials. Additionally, there is always the possibility of a poor harvest that could cause at least regional famine.

In terms of social developments, the prospects appear similarly bleak. Even if greater economic progress is achieved by the year 2000 than is currently predicted, at least 60 percent of the populace will still live in the hamlets, villages, and small towns of the countryside, and between 45 and 50 percent will still derive most of their income from farming. Both in the cities and in the villages, income differentials will most probably grow wider, and so will the gap between urban and rural income as well as the gap between the poor and the well-to-do regions.

Yet despite Karl Marx's assumption that developments in the social and economic base determine developments in the ideological and political "superstructure," the history of the PRC strongly suggests that the reverse is true: economic and social change depends upon political

---

[35]This figure was first published by a journalist from the ROC on Taiwan after intensive research in the PRC, in *CKSP*, September 21, 1989. Later, PRC officials revealed there were 1.8 million illegal childbirths in the year 1988.

developments. It is, therefore, of central importance to try to forecast possible political trends during the next decade in the PRC. We will do this by developing and analyzing alternative projections.

Theoretically, one projection could assume that the ruling elite is successful in its attempt to stifle dissent, and that this assures the evolution of a stable system of bureaucratic socialism. In this case, the ruling elite would continue to pursue its policy of a selective and controlled opening toward the outside world, but it would freeze domestic economic reforms at the 1988 level. Yet the evolution of a stable, institutionalized system of bureaucratic socialism, which means the continuation of Marxist-Leninist single-party rule well into the next century, has, since the Spring Crisis of 1989, become a very shaky foundation on which to build major strategy options for international politics. To assume an indefinite continuation of communist rule in China is a delusion, and it would be unwise to base projections about the political future of China on such a scenario.

The future of communist single-party rule in China is fairly easy to predict: New crises will deepen the rift and sharpen the contradiction between the rulers and the people, and between the party and society. Since the Beijing massacre of June 4, 1989, this gap has become unbridgeable. The outlook for the PRC political system points unmistakably toward a collapse of the communist system, yet it is by no means clear how long the agony of Marxist-Leninist rule may last. An examination of the political trends that may develop during the 1990s on the mainland of China can be accomplished through alternative projections, presented in the following four scenarios:

First, the scenario of a relatively long-term, though fragile, stabilization of the structures of domestic control. This would require a long period of repression under a predominantly orthodox leadership, which would probably be accompanied by corruption and an expansion of the parallel underground economy. But it would also mean freezing or rolling back to 1988 levels advances made in the fields of individual enterprises, state enterprise autonomy, and decollectivized agricultural production. Demands to move ahead in these areas would be refused by the ruling elite, and in order to sustain this refusal, the bureaucratic elements of the economy would have to be strengthened. As a consequence, social tensions would further increase and eventually explode in violent dissent. The ruling elite could probably stifle dissent for a while, but ultimately the confrontation in China would turn into a large-scale, extremely violent conflict, which would lead to the drowning of communist rule in a veritable ocean of blood.

18

Second, the scenario of a return of reform-oriented revisionists, who would be able to gain control of the decisionmaking organs of party and state. In this case, the new leadership would try to push ahead with thoroughgoing economic reforms, including the decontrolling of most prices, the decollectivization of rural land-ownership, the lifting of most, if not all, limitations on individual enterprise, and the granting of broader autonomy to public enterprises. Such daring reforms would be accompanied by political changes: an extension of direct elections from the county, where it stands today, to the provincial and, ultimately, the national level; the granting of considerable autonomy to social organizations; and the introduction of a free choice among several candidates in elections. But since the expansion of economic reforms would in all likelihood result in high inflation rates and a further increase in income differentials, the CCP would have to bear the brunt of public discontent with economic and social difficulties. This, in turn, would gradually dislodge the party from power—a situation somewhat similar to that in Poland today—and, hence, ensure a comparatively peaceful transition from the communist to a more pluralistic political system.

Third, the scenario of a return of reform-oriented revisionists, who would assume control of the decisionmaking organs of party and state and start to develop policies of economic and political reform. Yet, such policies would prompt a backlash from the orthodox forces, more likely than not in the form of a coup d'etat sanctioned by factions in the PLA. Such a coup would then provoke reaction from society in the form of a nationwide revolutionary movement which, with the support of other groups in the PLA, would finally result in a violent overthrow of communist rule.

Fourth, the scenario of a leadership crisis which will follow the death of Deng Xiaoping, Chen Yun, and other veteran revolutionaries, possibly coupled with a swift aggravation of the current economic crisis. Under these circumstances, which could develop earlier than most observers expect, the opposition forces in society would rise again on an even larger scale than they did in the spring of 1989. Faced with this intense opposition, many members of the PLA would no longer be willing to protect the rulers and fight the people, resulting in the disintegration of control structures and the whole system of CCP rule. The transition to another political system would be accomplished without large-scale bloodshed, leaving China under the rule of noncommunist elites well before the end of this century.

It is extremely difficult to attach a probability rating to each of these four scenarios. Yet given the scope of the de-legitimization of CCP rule in the Spring Crisis of 1989, the strong swell of popular discontent, and the current composition of the ruling elite, one can assign a greater probability to the first and the fourth scenarios than to the second and the third, and of the latter two, the third appears somewhat more probable than the second.

If either the first or the fourth scenario should develop, the world should be prepared for the rise of a new, noncommunist China—within the next two to five years, in the case of the fourth scenario, or early in the second decade of the twenty-first century, in the case of the first.

But what might follow the period of communist rule over China? Judging from the present status, there are two possible alternatives. One is the beginning of a long period marked by considerable regional autonomy, if not independence, of four to seven major regions of the country. This would not, however, mean a return to a system of "warlordism," as has frequently been suggested by many observers over recent years, but rather the emergence of a commonwealth-type network of several Chinese states. The other possible outcome is the formation of a coalition consisting of revolutionary elites from the mainland of China, the ruling elite of the Republic of China (ROC) on Taiwan, and the political and intellectual elites of Hong Kong. This coalition would initiate the transition to a pluralistic representative system which would guarantee freedom of speech, information, association, and assembly, gradually introduce a rule of law, and endorse competitive elections. This would be the implementation of the platform which the Democracy Movement developed during the spring of 1989.

In this context, it would be a serious mistake to underrate the role of the ROC on Taiwan. We can dismiss the possibility of a military intervention on the mainland by Taiwan in the event of a crisis in the PRC. But many observers of the Chinese political scene tend to underestimate the role that the ROC's alternative political system could have on political development in the PRC. The process of pluralization and incipient democratization of the political system in Taiwan has strongly influenced the quest for democracy in the PRC. The ROC is not going to "return to the mainland" to seize control after the collapse of communist rule. If this collapse should come about, those who will have engineered it will definitely not bow to the current government in Taipei. But the ROC has legal codes to offer, including rather liberal laws on political parties and the press. It also has in place highly trained administrative and managerial personnel and an educational system that, by comparison with the PRC system, is quite advanced. With these strengths, it seems obvious that the ROC on Taiwan will be an important factor in any political equation for China after the end of CCP rule.

This effort to predict the unfolding of political dynamics in the PRC during the 1990s and beyond should end on a note of caution. While the representative democracies throughout the world were impressed by the extent to which the Democracy Movement in the spring of 1989 shared their values, they and their citizens should be aware that the evolution of a democratic political system is not the only alternative to communist rule in the PRC. Nativistic or even atavistic alternatives could develop, which might result in replacing communist totalitarian rule with a totalitarian rule of a different, perhaps fascist or traditionalist, persuasion.

Consequences

Governments, business circles, and the general public in the countries of the democratic world should not assume that they have already won the sympathy and support of the future China. Even after communist rule ends in China, the political West in general, and the United States in particular, will have to strive for a close and mutually beneficial relationship with the newly emerging political system (or systems) in China. If the governments and business firms of Western countries, in a short-sighted effort to please the PRC's current leaders, decide to conduct business-as-usual with the ruling elite of the PRC today, they might well lose touch with the future of China.

The PRC will play only a marginal role in international politics during the next decade because of its domestic difficulties. Beijing cannot be used by the United States as a counterbalance against whatever opponent we may perceive in any international system based on confrontation, competition, or cooperation. Today, the PRC's role in international politics appears to be highly overestimated. She may need our support desperately, but we do not need hers.

Recognizing these facts, we should try to keep open as many gates into China as possible without compromising our support for change. It is most important for us to remember that China as a country is not identical with the current ruling elite of the PRC; our task must be to devise strategies to continue and deepen our contacts with the forces that will shape the future. If the Western powers concentrate their efforts on this task, they may be able to win the cooperation and even the friendship of twenty-first-century China, and that should be a foremost goal for policymakers today.

China's Global Strategic Perspectives on the Third World

by Chen Qimao

The concept of the "third world" emerged after World War II, when a tempestuous movement of national liberation swept over Asia, Africa, and Latin America. Several dozen nations rid themselves of the colonialist yoke and gained national independence. The concept began to take shape during the middle of the 1950s when some observers pinned the label "third world" on those newly independent nationalist countries that were outside the Western capitalist camp and the socialist camp. China has paid special attention to unity and cooperation with the third world, but it was not until the 1970s that the Chinese leaders and press began to use the expression. This does not mean, of course, that before the 1970s they had ignored national liberation movements in Asia, Africa, and Latin America, and those nationalist countries comprising the third world. In reality, even before the People's Republic of China was founded in 1949, Chinese communist leaders had already taken notice of Asia, Africa, and Latin America, a vast strategic area with a deep reservoir of revolutionary strength. After the founding of the PRC, their views on the third world underwent a process of change with the unfolding of world events.

From Realism to Romanticism, and Back to Realism: The Development of China's Outlook on the Third World

For a long period, from the early postwar days through the 1950s, Chinese communist leaders regarded the third world as an "intermediate zone" between the United States and the Soviet Union, and viewed the national liberation movement in Asia, Africa, and Latin America as one of the newly emerging, significant forces combating imperialism and colonialism. In August 1946, questioned in an interview by American journalist Anna Louise Strong whether it was possible for the United States to launch an anti-Soviet war, Mao Zedong replied: "The United States and the Soviet Union are separated by a vast zone which includes many capitalist, colonial, and semi-colonial countries in Europe, Asia and

Africa."[1] He thought that the United States could not possibly attack the Soviet Union before subduing those countries.

In the 1950s, after numerous Asian and African countries had won independence and the first Asian-African conference had been held in Bandung, Indonesia, in April 1955, with no colonial powers present, the postwar national liberation movement gained considerable momentum. Chinese leaders more and more regarded the third world as an independent and increasingly important force in the international arena. In early 1957, in an analysis of the Suez Crisis, Mao Zedong said:

> In the Middle East, two kinds of contradictions and three kinds of forces are in conflict. The two kinds of contradictions are: first, those between different imperialist powers, that is, between the United States and Britain and between the United States and France; and, second, those between the imperialist powers and the oppressed nations. The three kinds of forces are: one, the United States, the biggest imperialist power; two, Britain and France, second-rate imperialist powers; and three, the oppressed nations. Asia and Africa are today the main area of imperialist contention. National independence movements have emerged in these regions.[2]

In the early 1960s, as the national liberation movement in Asia, Africa, and Latin America grew stronger and President de Gaulle pursued an independent policy in Europe, Chinese leaders thought of the intermediate zone as being comprised of two parts, namely the first and second intermediate zones; the former consisted of those countries in Asia, Africa, and Latin America that either were independent already or were striving to win independence, while the latter consisted of the capitalist nations of Western Europe, Oceania, as well as Canada.[3] The composition of the first intermediate zone thus is nearly identical to that of the third world.

The development of international affairs during the last four decades has demonstrated that the idea of the intermediate zone put forward by the Chinese Communist Party (CCP) in the early postwar days was in accord with reality. However, during the 1960s Chinese leaders gradually formed some new perspectives on international affairs, including some unrealistic and romantic ideas about the third world.

In "Proposals for the International Communist Movement," a 1963 document reflecting its views on contemporary world events, the CCP

---

[1] *Selected works of Mao Tsetung*, Vol. IV (Beijing: People's Press, 1964), p.1191.

[2] Ibid., Vol. V (1977), p.341.

[3] "All the Anti-U.S. Imperialism Forces United," *People's Daily*, editorial, January 21, 1964.

noted that the vast region of "Asia, Africa and Latin America [is] where various contradictions of the current world are concentrated, and where imperialist rule is the weakest. It is the major region to see the world revolutionary storm combating imperialism directly."[4] In the same year, a joint editorial entitled "An Apologist for New Colonialism," published by the *People's Daily* and the magazine *Red Flag* added: "Currently, Asia, Africa, and Latin America are seeing an excellent situation of revolution. The national liberation movement in Asia, Africa, and Latin America is the most significant force combating imperialism directly."[5]

From then on, such arguments were repeatedly cited and interpreted in official speeches and press articles. In 1965, a pamphlet entitled *Long Live the Victory of People's War!* and published in the name of Lin Biao, then Defense Minister, stated:

Taking the globe as a whole, if North America and Western Europe can be called the "cities of the world," then Asia, Africa, and Latin America constitute "the rural areas of the world." Since World War II, the proletarian revolutionary movement has for various reasons been temporarily held back in the North American and West European capitalist countries, while the people's revolutionary movement in Asia, Africa, and Latin America has been growing vigorously. In a sense, the contemporary world revolution also presents a picture of the encirclement of cities by the rural areas.[6]

This statement implies that the world revolution can be promoted by relying on the encirclement of "the cities of the world" (North America and Western Europe) by "the rural areas of the world" (Asia, Africa, and Latin America).

Thanks to the efforts of third world countries, the Twenty-sixth General Assembly of the United Nations in 1971 adopted a resolution giving China's UN seat to the People's Republic of China. The editorial by the *People's Daily* on that occasion declared that "We stand firmly by the third world."[7] From then on the term "third world" appeared regularly in the Chinese press. In a political report on August 23, 1973, at the Tenth CCP Congress, Zhou Enlai said, "The awakening and growing strength of the third world is a significant event in current international relations."[8]

---

[4]Quoted from the CCP Central Committee's reply to the CPSU Central Committee; see *The Polemics on the General Line of the International Communist Movement* (Beijing: People's Press, 1965), p.13.

[5]Ibid., p. 217.

[6]*Red Flag*, No. 10, 1965.

[7]"On the 26th UN Assembly," *People's Daily*, editorial, December 27, 1971.

[8]*Documents of the 10th Congress of the CCP* (Beijing: People's Press, 1973), p.21.

It was the first time that the concept of the third world had been used in a CCP or Chinese government document.

In February 1974, during a talk with Zambia's President Kaunda, Mao Zedong set forth his strategic thinking on the three worlds. Two months later, Deng Xiaoping made a systematic interpretation of Mao Zedong's thoughts at the Sixth Special Session of the UN General Assembly.

> In this situation of "great disorder under heaven," all the political forces in the world have undergone drastic division and realignment through prolonged trials of strength and struggle. . . . Judging from the changes in international relations, the world today actually consists of three parts, or three worlds, that are both interconnected and in contradiction to one another. The United States and the Soviet Union make up the first world. The developing countries in Asia, Africa, Latin America, and other regions make up the third world. The developed countries between the two make up the second world.[9]

In speaking of the developing countries, he pointed out:

> These countries cover vast territories, encompass a large population, and abound in natural resources. Having suffered the heaviest oppression, they have the strongest desire to oppose oppression and seek liberation and development. . . . They constitute a revolutionary driving force propelling the wheel of world history and are the main force combating colonialism, imperialism, and particularly the superpowers.[10]

Finally, he affirmed that "China belongs to the third world." Thus, China's viewpoint on the third world was formed theoretically and systematically, and China consistently adhered to it until the end of the 1970s.

It was obviously right for China to praise the third world's awakening and resurgence, and to stress the significance of the solidarity and struggle of these countries. However, after the world entered the mid-1960s, the high tide of the national liberation movement was over; the overwhelming majority of third world countries, having won their independence, stepped into the era of national economic development in order to consolidate their political independence. Peace and development gradually replaced war and revolution as the hallmarks of the times. Under these circumstances, it would not have been accurate to continue emphasizing that a strong revolutionary situation existed in Asia, Africa, and Latin America, or that these regions represented the center of the world revolutionary storm buffeting imperialism, or that they were the main force combating imperialism, colonialism, and hegemonism. Actually,

---

[9] *People's Daily*, April 11, 1974.
[10] Ibid.

the situation in which "the rural areas of the world" were to have encircled "the cities of the world" never materialized. With the victories and the maturation of the national independence movement, the revolutionary storm in the third world tended to calm down while the contradictions inside and among third world countries became manifest.

How could such unrealistic estimates be made? Objectively, it was because of the continuing rise and fall of the national liberation movements in Africa, Asia, and Latin America. Although overall they were losing momentum, occasionally there would be a resurgence, as occurred in the early 1970s: the victory of North Vietnam against the South and its ally, the United States; the fourth Middle East war; the oil embargo by Arab countries; the development of the struggle against colonialism and racism in Africa; Latin America's struggle to defend its maritime zone; and the emergence of various organizations in the third world, such as the Conference of Heads of State and Government of Non-Aligned Countries, the Organization of African Unity, the Arab League, the Organization of the Islamic Conference, the Association of Southeast Asian Nations (ASEAN), and so on. These gave rise to expectations and illusions as well. Subjectively, mistakes were made because of the gradual increase of incorrect thinking of the leftist tendency inside the Chinese Communist Party, starting at the end of the 1950s, which caused the leaders to deviate to some extent from the guidelines based on scientific materialism when they sought to interpret international events.

After the Third Plenary Session of the Eleventh Central Committee of the CCP in November 1978, Chinese leaders reappraised the world situation and made a systematic adjustment of Chinese foreign policies for the 1980s, including changes in China's views on, and relations with, the third world, which may be summarized as follows:

(1) They reiterated that "the emergence of the third world on the international arena is an event of primary importance in our times,"[11] and that "their joint struggle has, to a great extent, changed the situation in which the superpowers could arbitrarily manipulate the destiny of the world."[12] But there was no reference to the third world as the main force combating imperialism, colonialism, and hegemonism.

---

[11]Hu Yaobang's report at the CCP's 12th Congress, September 1, 1982, in the *Survey of International Affairs 1983* (hereafter referred to as *Survey*) (Shanghai: China Encyclopaedia Press, 1983), p. 368.

[12]Huang Hua's speech at 27th UN Assembly, October 10, 1982, in ibid., p. 379.

(2)   They stressed that "the development of the third world is an important factor for strengthening the forces of world peace,"[13]   but dropped all reference to the third world as a driving force of revolution, or as "the major region to see the world revolutionary storm combating imperialism directly."

(3)   They asserted that "many third world countries have stepped onto another historical stage at which the central assignment is to develop their national economies,"[14]   and that "mutual assistance among third world countries will be of prime importance." They declared that China supports the third world countries in their struggle to establish a new international economic order.[15]

(4)   They affirmed that the general principles underlying China's foreign policy are: "to strive to strengthen solidarity and cooperation with the third world countries; to develop friendly relations with all countries of the world on the basis of the Five Principles of Peaceful Coexistence";[16] and "to oppose hegemonism firmly and safeguard world peace."   They emphasized that "China is a member of the third world,"[17] and that "the fundamental foothold of its foreign policy is to strengthen solidarity and cooperation with the third world countries."[18]

The modifications imply that China has given up some unrealistic ideas about the third world and has returned to realism. After the Third Plenary Session of the Eleventh Central Committee of the CCP, Chinese leaders corrected the ideological line and systematically eliminated the incorrect left-leaning ideology. This has resulted in a new, more realistic analysis of international affairs which affirms that the main theme of the current era is no longer war and revolution but peace and development. The open policy since 1979 has also made it possible for China to conduct an overall and systematic assessment of the current status of the world. Since the second half of the 1970s, the developments in the third world have been characterized by the following developments: the tide of the national liberation movement has receded except in a few areas; after

---

[13]Deng Xiaoping on World Situation, May 1985, in *Survey 1986*, p. 265.

[14]Zhao Ziyang's report on the Government Work at the Second Session of the 6th Chinese People's Congress, in *Survey 1985*, p. 275.

[15]Hu Yaobang's report at the CCP's 12th Congress, in *Survey 1983*, p. 372.

[16]The Five Principles of Peaceful Coexistence are mutual respect for sovereignty and territorial integrity, non-aggression, non-interference in internal affairs, equality and mutual benefit, and peaceful coexistence.

[17]Zhao Ziyang's report, *Survey 1985*, p. 270.

[18]Zhao Ziyang's report on the Government Work at the First Session of the 6th Chinese People's Congress, in *Survey 1984*, p.417.

entering the new stage of developing their national economies, the majority of developing countries have been faced with economic difficulties; conflicts and contradictions among developing countries have increased; South-South cooperation has not seen much progress; divisions have emerged inside the third world, resulting in different blocs of countries, such as "newly industrializing" countries and regions, petroleum producers, medium- and low-income countries. The tendency of third world countries to take joint actions has been weakened. All of these developments have made China more sober-minded in its assessment of the third world.

Problems, Trends, and Countermeasures: An Analysis of Various Areas in the Third World

Northeast Asia

Thirty-seven years have elapsed since the armistice ending the fighting in the Korean War, but up to now the tensions of military confrontation between the North and the South remain. On the two sides of the DMZ, 1.4 million troops are under arms, of which the North has 800,000 and the South 600,000, not counting 40,000 U.S. troops. Both sides are equipped with advanced military weapons provided by the two superpowers, and the U.S. troops stationed in South Korea are equipped with tactical nuclear weapons. This major military confrontation has for many years made the Korean Peninsula the world's second largest powderkeg next to Central Europe. The North-South dialogue began in July 1972, but for various reasons progress is very slow and it has failed to eliminate tensions in the peninsula.

Despite the sharp contradictions between the two Korean states, they share common views on peaceful reunification. In a joint statement in July 1972, the North and the South affirmed that the three principles of self-determination, peace, and promotion of national unity transcended their differences in thinking, beliefs, and systems. These three principles were endorsed by the 28th General Assembly of the United Nations in November 1973. Since then, despite many setbacks and suspensions of bilateral talks, both sides in the North-South dialogue have consistently recognized the three principles. This at least keeps alive hopes of a final peaceful reunification in the Korean Peninsula.

The current situation is favorable to the reconciliation of North and South, because it appears to be in the interests of both sides. North Korea has experienced some difficulties in its economic development in recent years; meanwhile, the economy of South Korea is growing at a high rate, producing a per capita GNP in 1988 of over 4,000 U.S. dollars.[19] The gap between the two countries has been widening for many years. Moreover, the success of the Olympic Games in Seoul has improved South Korea's international status. Faced with this situation, North Korea is in urgent need of a peaceful and stable environment so as to concentrate its energy on economic development. President Kim Il Sung has asserted again and again that North Korea has neither the intention nor the ability to drive southwards. In South Korea, one-fourth of its population and 50 percent of its industry and GNP are concentrated in Seoul, a city close to the armistice line which can easily be destroyed in the event of a war. For the sake of stability and further development of its economy, South Korea also strongly desires an improvement of bilateral relations. Meanwhile, in order to maintain a stable environment in the Asian-Pacific region, the Soviet Union, the United States, China, and Japan, the big powers concerned with the peninsula, also want to see a relaxation of tensions instead of a renewal of war. Under these circumstances, it is possible that the North-South dialogue may achieve breakthroughs on some fronts.

Nevertheless, in the foreseeable future, it is unlikely that Korea will make much progress toward reunification. North Korea has raised the suggestion that each side should keep its respective state system but join together in a federation that would adopt a unified name. Neither would annex the other. This is feasible in theory; but in reality, because of the long-standing partition and separation, the serious estrangement and suspicion of the two sides cannot be eliminated over the short run. In view of the fact that the politics of both states are in a transitional period at present, and both have some destabilizing internal problems, no major steps can be taken before the process of succession is completed and before the new power structures are consolidated. Thus, peaceful reunification on the basis of self-determination will be a very long process and may only be realized in the next century.

Both halves of Korea and the countries concerned agree that the primary task at the moment is to relax tensions in the Korean Peninsula and to maintain peace and stability there. To attain these objectives, the following measures may be helpful:

(1) Promote nongovernmental exchanges in economics, culture, sports, and other fields, allow cross-border visits by family members and relatives on both sides, and provide for mail service and trade. For these purposes, the two sides should revise their respective laws and

---

[19]Announced by the Bank of (South) Korea in March 1988; quoted by French News Agency, Seoul, May 9, 1988.

regulations that hinder such exchanges and, at the same time, each side should stop engaging in espionage against the other side.

(2) Improve exchanges and contacts between the United States, Japan, and North Korea, and between China, the Soviet Union, and South Korea. In this respect, the initiatives of the United States are of great importance.

(3) Arrange for the withdrawal of U.S. troops from South Korea on a step-by-step basis. As a first step, the United States should end or at least suspend the joint Team Spirit military maneuvers with South Korean troops, thereby creating a favorable atmosphere for North-South dialogue. The armistice in Korea has lasted for 37 years and important changes have taken place in Sino-U.S. relations and Soviet-U.S. relations. But the United States still stations troops on the Korean Peninsula and puts South Korean troops under the command of a U.S. general. This anachronistic situation not only presents an obstacle to the relaxation of tensions in the Korean Peninsula, but also seriously hurts the self-esteem of the South Korean people, and gives rise to increasing anti-Americanism which is not in the interests of the United States itself.

(4) Decrease gradually the level of military forces on both sides of the armistice line through negotiations between the North, the United States, and the South, and substitute a peace treaty for the existing armistice agreement when conditions warrant.

Southeast Asia

The Kampuchea issue is still the primary problem facing Southeast Asian countries at present. The 1989 Paris ministerial session on Kampuchea has come to a close, with limited results. A political solution of the Kampuchean issue was not reached, and the situation remains complicated. The people of Kampuchea and the international community hope that national reconciliation can be achieved, and that general elections can be held so that Kampuchea will become an independent, peaceful, and neutral country, after the complete withdrawal of Vietnamese troops. But judging from the current situation, there are three possible, dangerous outcomes: (1) The Khmer Rouge could assume power alone. (2) Following the same disastrous road taken in Afghanistan, a civil war may break out after the withdrawal of Vietnamese troops. (3) Backed by Vietnam, and drawing on a certain faction in the coalition government of democratic Kampuchea, the Phnom Penh regime could set up a new government with itself as the dominant force, and thus the reins of power would be held by one faction.

During its rule, the Khmer Rouge made serious mistakes and inflicted disaster upon the Kampuchean people. The worries and anxieties in the international community about the Khmer Rouge regaining power are understandable. But in reality there is little chance that the Khmer Rouge can take power by itself. Although the Khmer Rouge armed force is the strongest of the resistance forces, they have been severely criticized abroad and are in an isolated position. The people of Kampuchea have lingering fears about them. The Chinese government has clearly stated that China, together with other countries, will halt its military assistance to any faction in Kampuchea whenever a comprehensive agreement is reached and Vietnam withdraws all of its troops under international supervision. Repeatedly, China has declared that it does not support a Khmer Rouge effort to seize power alone. It is hardly conceivable that the Khmer Rouge could regain power without internal and external support. Hence, this danger is greatly exaggerated.

The two other dangerous outcomes are more plausible: One is that Kampuchea falls into disintegration, becoming another Afghanistan or Lebanon. The other is that the Phnom Penh regime takes power alone.

Some intelligence shows that 50,000 to 70,000 Vietnamese army troops have disguised themselves as troops and militia of the Phnom Penh regime. This would indicate that Vietnam is not giving up its plan for an Indochina federation, and is still trying to control Kampuchea after its superficial withdrawal. It is reported that the military forces of the Phnom Penh regime have been greatly strengthened in recent years. It now has regular and local troops numbering 100,000, with considerable strength in the militia.[20] Supported by invading Vietnamese troops, the Phnom Penh regime has actually taken control of all cities and most of the territory of Kampuchea. In all likelihood, in collusion with each other, Vietnam and the Phnom Penh regime are going to divide and demoralize the resistance forces, set up a new government with the Heng Samrin and Hun Sen faction as its dominant element, and thus take power by itself. One important aspect of this plot is deliberately to exaggerate the danger of the Khmer Rouge regaining power and to try their best to exclude the Khmer Rouge from a provisional government. If this plot succeeds, it means all the efforts of the Kampuchean resistance forces against the Vietnamese invasion will be irrevocably lost, and the just struggle of the international community against the Vietnamese invasion of Kampuchea will fail.

In order to preempt the above dangers and enable Kampuchea to

---

[20] *Far East Economic Review*, June 29, 1989.

overcome present difficulties and take an independent, peaceful, neutral, and prosperous road, the most important measures that need to be taken now are: (1) Placing the withdrawal of Vietnamese troops under effective international supervision, to guarantee they are actually withdrawn and to prevent them from holding on to the territory of Kampuchea in disguise. (2) Dissolving the Phnom Penh regime and the coalition government of democratic Kampuchea, establishing a provisional coalition government headed by Prince Sihanouk, reducing equally the number of troops each faction is permitted to field, and stipulating that the army is prohibited from participating in politics and interfering in elections, thereby assuring that the Kampuchean people can take part in free elections without external interference and threats of force. In this way restrictions can be imposed on both the Phnom Penh regime and the Khmer Rouge, and a civil war can be prevented.

If the Kampuchean issue is properly solved, not only can Indochina rid itself of the long turmoil of war and begin to concentrate on economic development, but the entire Southeast Asian region will be in a more favorable position for achieving peace, stability, and economic progress. However, quite a few destabilizing problems remain for Southeast Asia:

(1) There exist complicated class and racial contradictions and religious disputes within the Southeast Asian countries. In some of them (e.g., the Philippines and Burma), wars between government forces and communist parties or religious forces are still going on. At present, most Southeast Asian countries have entered a transitional period: the leaders of the immediate postwar generation have stepped down or will soon step down from the political stage and will be succeeded by people from a new generation who have come of age in the postwar years. The process of economic development has produced new social groups, which want greater political participation and democratization. In this process, it is unavoidable that they will come into conflict with conservative forces. If these problems are not properly handled, unrest may occur. One must hope that most Southeast Asian countries will achieve political democratization and replace old political power structures with new ones, without grave turmoil.

(2) Seizing the opportunity created by Vietnam's invasion of Kampuchea, the Soviet Union strengthened its military bases and deployed permanent naval and air forces in Cam Ranh Bay. Facing each other across the South China Sea, the Soviet bases in Vietnam and U.S. bases in the Philippines have turned Southeast Asian waters into a new arena of military competition and rivalry between the superpowers, and thus increased uneasiness among the countries and peoples of Southeast Asia. In September 1988 in Krasnoyarsk, Gorbachev

suggested that the Soviet Union would be willing to dismantle its military bases in Cam Ranh Bay if the United States dismantled its military bases in the Philippines. The United States dismissed the suggestion as unrealistic. Building up its military bases in Cam Ranh Bay is a glaring example of the Soviet "southward drive policy" of the Brezhnev era. The dismantling of the bases there would be a clear sign that the Soviet Union not only in words but in deeds is moving toward a defensive strategy. The lease of U.S. military bases in the Philippines will expire in 1991, and whether it will be renewed or the bases transferred elsewhere in the area depends on the struggles among different factions within the Philippines, the outcome of U.S.-Philippine negotiations, and the attitudes of the Southeast Asian countries. The diminishing military rivalry in Southeast Asia between the United States and the Soviet Union will doubtlessly be helpful to peace and stability in this region.

(3) Disputes over claims to islands and maritime rights in the South China Sea have become conspicuous in recent years. The Nansha Islands (Spratly Islands) has been China's territory since the fourteenth century.[21] It was occupied by Japan for a time during the Second World War, and was retaken by the Chinese government after the war with no international objections. Before 1974, Vietnam also admitted that Nansha is China's territory. But after 1975, Vietnam occupied some twenty small Nansha islands. Meanwhile, the Philippines and Malaysia also occupied some of the Nansha islands. On March 14, 1988, the Chinese Navy sank two Vietnamese naval ships off Nansha. Once the Kampuchean issue is solved, Nansha may become the new center of contention. China claims that Nansha is Chinese sovereign territory. But in order to maintain peace and stability in the Asia-Pacific region, China insists on solving disputes through peaceful negotiations. In view of the current situation, China suggests that for now the problem of Nansha might be shelved; as a first step, the dispute might be eased through joint exploration and exploitation of resources by the concerned parties. Under this policy, China would agree to discuss with the countries involved a solution to the problem. But in April 1988, Vietnam declared Nansha to be under the administration of its Phu Khanh province.[22] China can never tolerate such an action.

After the Kampuchea issue is solved, China will strive further to develop good neighborly relations with Southeast Asian countries. China always

---

[21]Cf PRC Foreign Ministry's Memorandum on Xisha and Nansha Islands, May 12, 1988, in *Survey 1989*, p. 297.

[22]Vietnam Foreign Ministry Document, *Huangsha Islands, Changsha Islands, and International Law*, April 1988. The Huangsha Islands are the same as China's Xisha islands, and the Changsha islands are China's Nansha islands.

supports ASEAN in its efforts to work for peace, stability, and economic development in the region. China normalized relations with Indonesia in August 1990 and expects to establish diplomatic relations with Singapore and Brunei as well. China has for a long time halted its material assistance to communists in Southeast Asian countries. Beijing encourages overseas Chinese in Southeast Asian countries to acquire the nationality of their resident countries on a voluntary basis and asks those who retain Chinese citizenship to abide by the laws of the resident countries, respect local customs and habits, and live in friendship with the local people. Time will prove that the "Sinophobia" in Southeast Asian countries is totally groundless.

South Asia

Afghanistan remains the major source of instability in South Asia. The struggle between the Afghan resistance forces and the Kabul regime has been intensified since the withdrawal of Soviet troops. Taking advantage of the Soviet withdrawal, the Afghan seven-party alliance based in Pakistan thought it would be able to capture the big cities such as Kabul and Jalalabad, wipe out government troops, and seize state power in swift order. However, since Soviet troops were withdrawn in mid-February 1989, resistance forces, despite suffering heavy casualties, have been unable to take Jalalabad. The civil war remains deadlocked. Government troops and resistance forces seem to be well matched in strength, so that neither side can defeat the other. If this situation continues, it will result in prolonged turmoil and warfare, and plunge the Afghan people into greater suffering.

Afghanistan is still a country of tribal dominance, with more than 3,000 tribes, big and small. The solution to the Afghanistan problem cannot but proceed from this reality. To achieve internal peace and solve the problem of repatriating and settling five million refugees, a more realistic approach at present would be to establish a broad-based coalition government comprising all parties and headed by some neutral Afghans acceptable to all; permit all parties under this government to set up autonomous local governments in areas under their control; and with international guarantees make Afghanistan an independent, neutral, and nonaligned country. The United Nations is intensifying its efforts to mediate the dispute. The Soviet Union has given up its plan of setting up a coalition government with the People's Democratic Party of Afghanistan as the leading partner, while the Kabul regime has expressed its willingness to take part in a coalition government as one of the parties. The United States, although supporting the resistance forces, actually would prefer not to have the fundamentalists, currently occupying the dominant position in the resistance movement, hold the reins of government. China has explicitly expressed its wish that all Afghan parties reach a compromise and establish a broad-based government acceptable to all. Pakistan has supported the Afghan seven-party alliance's bid to take power, but now shows an inclination to favor political settlement. The seven-party alliance unilaterally formed a provisional government, not yet recognized by the international community, which only deepened the differences among the resistance forces. Because the seven-party alliance has been unable to win a military victory, moderates within its ranks may gain strength. For all of these reasons, it may be possible to achieve a compromise settlement and form a coalition government.

In addition to the Afghanistan problem, there are other widespread national, territorial, and religious conflicts in the region, such as the Pakistani-Indian territorial dispute over Jammu and Kashmir, the disagreement between India and Sri Lanka about the withdrawal of Indian troops from Sri Lanka, Nepali-Indian differences over trade routes, the Sino-Indian dispute over their border territory, and others. Moreover, there are complicated religious and racial problems within some South Asian countries.

The root causes underlying the disputes and conflicts among South Asian countries are:

(1) *Historic issues left behind by the colonial powers.* South Asia became a British colony or sphere of influence in the mid-nineteenth century. In the years leading to World War II, the British Empire had pursued a policy of divide and rule in South Asia and left behind numerous territorial and national disputes. The Pakistani-Indian territorial dispute is an example of this legacy of divide and rule.

(2) *The rising trend of regional hegemonism.* After independence, the ruling clique of India inherited to some extent the mantle of the British Empire and sought, as the largest country of South Asia, to hold sway over this region. In recent years, as the Indian economy developed and its military capabilities grew stronger, with Soviet assistance playing an important role, New Delhi's hegemonist aspirations grew. For example, in March 1989, against international convention, India cut off most of the trade routes between Nepal, a landlocked country, and other countries, and stopped exporting the necessities of life such as petroleum products and salt to Nepal. This is not merely an economic dispute, but a question of whether India can control Nepal's actions.

(3) *Involvement by the superpowers.* After World War II, U.S. influence replaced that of Britain in India, and the Soviet Union began to take an

active role in South Asian affairs in the late 1950s. In 1971, the Soviet Union and India signed a Treaty of Peace, Friendship, and Cooperation, essentially a military alliance to support India's expansion in the region. As its relations with India deteriorated, the United States put greater stress on supporting Pakistan, although it did not give up its bid for closer ties with India. The U.S.-USSR competition in South Asia has now continued for three decades, contributing to the contradictions and conflicts in the region.

In recent years, in the general international climate of detente, disputes between the South Asian countries have diminished. In December 1988, former Indian Prime Minister Rajiv Gandhi visited China. The governments of the two countries reached agreements in principle to restore and develop good neighborly relations on the basis of the Five Principles of Peaceful Coexistence and to settle the border question through peaceful and friendly consultation. While Benazir Bhutto was in power, the prime ministers of India and Pakistan met several times and relations between the two countries improved. The South Asian Association of Regional Cooperation set up in December 1985 has made some progress, but up to now, none of the disputes in this region has been settled. Some of these disputes may persist for a long time, and others may actually intensify and lead to conflict. Whether India can suppress the hegemonist tendencies of its foreign policy and settle its disputes with neighboring countries peacefully is still the key to peace and stability in South Asia.

Persian Gulf

Since Iran and Iraq accepted UN Resolution 598 on August 20, 1988, calling for a cease-fire, the two countries have been in a state of no peace-no war. The peace talks under the auspices of the UN Secretary-General are stalemated: Tehran insists that the two sides should first evacuate their troops to their own sides of the original border, while Baghdad maintains its position that the first priority is for Iran to clear the Shatt al Arab waterway and to agree to an exchange of POWs. The conflict of views is centered on the sovereignty over the Shatt al Arab waterway. Iran is adamant that both sides observe the Algiers Agreement signed in 1975, which set the demarcation line in the mid-channel of the Shatt al Arab waterway, whereas Iraq demands that the agreement be abolished, and that all sovereign rights to the waterway be recovered by Iraq. A compromise on this issue is unlikely. The possibility of renewed warfare cannot be ruled out; but given the heavy losses suffered by both countries in the eight-year-long war, the urgent need for recovery of their war-torn economies, declining public support for more bloodshed, and the changing international climate, the chances of a new conflict in the near future are slim.

Under the late religious leader Ayatollah Khomeini, the Iranian government strengthened its theocratic rule, exported Islamic revolution, and pursued a "no east and no west" policy. In February 1989, the Ayatollah's action in publicly passing the death sentence upon Rushdie, the British author of the novel *Satanic Verses*, shocked the West and caused further deterioration of relations between Western countries and Iran. Following Khomeini's demise, President Ali Khamenei succeeded him as religious leader, and Speaker Rafsanjani was elected president. Since the two represent the more pragmatic element in Iran's ruling circles, their coming to power indicates that the pragmatists have assumed dominant positions in the power structure of the country and that Iran will follow a comparatively moderate and practical line. In June 1989, Iran signed a series of comprehensive economic, science, and technological cooperation agreements with the Soviet Union, and in the recent hostage crisis in Lebanon, Rafsanjani made some flexible gestures. He has also declared that Iran will strive to improve its relations with its Gulf neighbors and other Arab countries. All of these changes should contribute to peace and stability in the Gulf region.

Both Iran and Iraq are powers in the Gulf area. Saudi Arabia, another Gulf power, formed a Gulf Cooperation Council—a regional economic cooperation and mutual defense organization—in February 1981 with Kuwait, Oman, United Arab Emirates, Bahrain, and Qatar. This tripartite balance of forces may well control Gulf politics for a long time to come.

In a region of strategic importance, the Gulf countries hold 55 percent of the proven reserves of the globe's oil. Of total oil consumption in the West in 1986, about 60 percent of Japan's, some 30 percent of Western Europe's, and roughly 8 percent of U.S. consumption came from the Gulf region. Overall, in the same year, about 17 percent of all oil consumed in the West was transiting the Strait of Hormuz. That is why, in the global strategy of the superpowers, the Gulf area is critical. Not long before his death, Ayatollah Khomeini, in order to lift Iran out of its isolation, displayed a willingness to improve relations with the Soviet Union, and Moscow seized the opportunity to send Foreign Minister Shevardnadze to Tehran in February 1989, and played host to the visiting Rafsanjani in June of the same year. Washington is also seeking opportunities to deal with Iran's new leaders. The superpower competition on the political and diplomatic level in the Gulf is not likely to diminish soon.

China maintains good relations with both Iran and Iraq. During the Gulf war, China time and again called on them to end the war, begin peace talks, and solve the territorial dispute through negotiations. In recent years, China has significantly improved its relations with Saudi Arabia, and both parties have agreed to set up trade representative's offices in each other's countries. In 1988, the Saudis turned to China for the sale of missiles and promised that they would be used only for defensive purposes and would not be transferred to other countries. When the Chinese government fulfilled the Saudi request, the United States condemned this arms sale as endangering the stability of the region, and Israel threatened to destroy the Saudi missile base because it posed an intolerable threat to Israeli security. Tel Aviv refrained from such reckless action only because of criticism from the Arab countries and strong objections from Washington.

The U.S. accusation against China is unwarranted, for it is well known that the United States and the Soviet Union are the world's biggest arms suppliers to the Gulf. China's arms exports to this region are insignificant compared with those of the United States, the Soviet Union, and the West European countries. In the balance of military might between Israel and Saudi Arabia, Israel is certainly the stronger. When Washington provides Tel Aviv with large quantities of sophisticated offensive weapons, and then blames the Saudis for buying a small amount of arms from China, one cannot help thinking of an old Chinese proverb: "The Magistrates are free to burn down houses while the common people are forbidden to light a lamp." China, which is usually very cautious in its approach toward arms trade, has set three principles to govern these transactions: they must be helpful to the receiver's legitimate right of self-defense; contribute to the maintenance and strengthening of regional peace, security, and stability; and promote non-interference in other countries' domestic affairs. China will act firmly in accordance with these principles in future arms sales.

Middle East

The term Middle East denotes West Asia and North Africa, including the Persian Gulf, but here I will focus on the Arab-Israeli conflicts. For more than forty years, the situation in this region has been complicated and turbulent; between the Arab countries and Israel alone, four comparatively large-scale wars have erupted. As a result of these conflicts, Israel occupied 71,700 square kilometers of land, including the Sinai Peninsula which has been returned to Egypt, and more than one and a half million Palestinians have fled their homeland and become refugees. All Arab countries, with the exception of Egypt, continue in a state of war with Israel. The Arab-Israeli conflict, the main contradiction in the Middle East, is a complex problem consisting of three main elements: (1) the Arab countries' demand for Israeli withdrawal from all territories occupied during the June 1967 war; (2) the Palestinian people's resolve to recover their national rights, including the rights to return to their homeland, to national self-determination, and to the establishment of a state; (3) the desire by both the Palestinian and Israeli peoples to achieve lasting peace and stability, so that their countries may be independent and secure.

The crux of the problem is how to solve the Palestine question. With the exception of the Golan Heights of Syria, all territories occupied by the Israelis—the West Bank, the Gaza Strip, and the Arab sector of Jerusalem—comprise the homeland of the Palestinians. Once the Palestinian question is solved, it should not be too difficult to reach a solution on an Israeli pullout from the Golan Heights. But only when the Palestinian question is solved can one talk about the independence and existence of all Middle East countries. Since the Palestinian uprising in the West Bank and Gaza Strip began in December 1987, over 500 people have been killed, making this question all the more urgent to solve.

Supported by the United States, relying on its military superiority, and using its threatened security as pretext, Israel has refused to withdraw from occupied lands and to restore Palestinian national rights, and has opposed the establishment of an independent Palestinian state. Israel's stubborn position has been the main obstacle to the settlement of Middle East problems.

In 1988 a favorable turn emerged in the course of negotiations on the Middle East problem. The PLO, after repeated discussions and overcoming internal differences, decided to choose the road of peace, accepted UN resolutions 242, 338, and 181, and declared the establishment of a Palestinian state. At the same time, it recognized Israel's right to exist. Soon after that, the United States, which had been urging the PLO to take these steps, decided to enter into a direct dialogue with the PLO. These moves have brought new hope for a peaceful settlement of Middle East problems. Now the problem is whether Israel can change its intransigent position. The Israelis have so far clung to their policy of no recognition of the PLO, no recognition of Palestinian rights to self-determination, no establishment of a Palestinian state, and no convening of an international Middle East peace conference. To date, Israel is willing only to allow the Palestinian people to exercise "limited self-rule" in the West Bank and Gaza. It is Israel's adamant position that stands in the way of achieving a breakthrough in settling Middle East problems.

During the Second World War, the Jews fell prey to Nazi genocide policies and millions of them were slaughtered. People around the world feel sympathetic toward them, and it is understandable that the Israelis feel particularly concerned about their own security. However, at present in the Middle East the problem is not that the Arab countries are denying Israel the right of existence, but rather that the Israelis are denying Palestinians their right of existence and self-determination in their homeland. This attitude of the Israeli government has long earned the Jewish state the hatred, hostility, and opposition of the Arab countries. This is not in the real long-term interests of the Israeli people. Only by changing its course, recognizing the Palestinian people's right of self-determination, settling disputes through negotiation, and co-existing with the Arab countries, can Israel truly assure its security.

In settling Middle East problems, U.S. policy plays a significant role. Since 1982, the United States has shifted its Middle East policy to some extent, but has not fundamentally modified its stand which favors Israel. On the Palestine problem, Washington has advocated a formula of settling the Palestinian problem in association with Jordan, without recognizing the Palestinian right of self-determination. The United States, instead of displaying partiality to Israel, should further adjust its Middle East policy by urging Israel to change its rigid position, and by taking advantage of the relatively favorable trends in the Middle East to achieve a breakthrough in that region's problems.

Since 1975, Lebanon has been partitioned by separatist religious sects and armed forces scrambling for power, resulting in endless war and turmoil. External powers, including Israel, Iran, and Syria—especially the latter with some 30,000 to 40,000 troops stationed there—have intervened and now control three-fourths of the country. At present, Lebanon with its paralyzed Assembly, assassinated presidents, parallel power structures, random violence, and factional strife has become the most chaotic country in the world. The chaos in Lebanon is inseparable from the problems in the Middle East, where serious contradictions abound: religious contradictions between Christianity and Islam; between different religious sects within these two great religions; among Arab countries, Palestine, and Israel; among various Arab countries; and between Arab countries and Iran, and so on. The Lebanon problem can be solved only in the process of a step-by-step settlement of wider Middle East problems. In May 1989, the Arab Summit decided to form a tripartite committee consisting of Algeria, Morocco, and Saudi Arabia to promote a cease-fire and presidential election in Lebanon. The international community should support their effort, and external forces, including those of Israel, Syria, and Iran, should withdraw from Lebanon so that the country may be able to find a formula of peaceful coexistence among the different religious sects. Perhaps a certain form of federation will provide a way out of this imbroglio.

Africa

In 1988, reflecting the superpower detente, there occurred a chain reaction of political settlements of various conflicts in Africa. Angola, Cuba, and South Africa, through arduous negotiations mediated by the United States and the Soviet Union, settled their differences and signed agreements providing for the independence of Namibia and the withdrawal of Cuban troops from Angola, thus ending the 13-year-long war in southwest Africa. Through the mediation of the Organization of African Unity (OAU), the Chad-Libyan conflict over Aozi has come to an end and diplomatic relations between the two countries have been resumed. Morocco and the Front de Polisario, backed by Algeria, have accepted the United Nations' proposal for a cease-fire, and the future of West Sahara—independence or annexation to Morocco—will be decided by a referendum under UN supervision. Ethiopia and Somalia, having fought several wars for Ogaden, also have resumed diplomatic relations through OAU mediation. Moreover, dialogues and peace talks between confronting parties in countries such as Mozambique, Sudan, Somalia, and Ethiopia have made notable progress.

In the wake of Namibian independence, the historic mission of the African national liberation movement has basically been fulfilled. What is left is racial discrimination in South Africa. Pressed by the struggle of the South African people (the blacks and the many whites who are against racial discrimination) and the international community, South African authorities are no longer able to continue at will their practice of racial discrimination which, sooner or later, will certainly be eliminated. The international community should seize the opportunity by putting more pressure on the South African government to move more swiftly to end apartheid. Realization of complete racial equality will be a long process and needs the unremitting efforts of all parties.

With the fulfillment of the mission of national liberation and independence, the critical tasks for most African countries are to achieve internal reconciliation, strengthen stability and unity, and promote economic development. Beginning in 1982, Africa was ravaged by a three- or four-year severe drought, which brought suffering and hunger to 150 million people; millions of them, including a great many children, died. In addition to the severe natural disasters, large areas of Africa are beset by external and internal conflicts, turmoil, and faulty economic policies. In recent years, the economic situation in Africa has turned for the better and the food crisis has been eased in some areas, but economic problems—especially in agriculture—in most African countries are still very serious. It is imperative for African countries to settle civil wars, disturbances, and international conflicts through negotiation, and seek a peaceful and stable environment so that they may be able to concentrate their resources on economic development, especially on strengthening agriculture, which is the foundation of a national economy. Priority must be given to the development of grain production and to controlling population growth. It is crucial for developed countries, especially those West European countries which have traditional ties with Africa, to help African countries with economic aid grants, qualified personnel, and transfer of technology.

Before independence, most African countries were in pre-capitalist stages; some were in a feudal condition, some under slavery, and others dominated by a primitive tribal system. After independence, but still in dire economic straits, some countries were influenced by the Soviet Union and blindly adopted radical measures of social reform, nationalization, and "socialism." These policies were generally counterproductive to economic development, and sometimes even created economic havoc. At the same time, some countries, such as the Ivory Coast, the Comoros, and Botswana, which relied on a capitalist market economy, developed their economies more rapidly. Experience shows that African countries are at present in a period of transition from pre-capitalism to capitalism, and that it is not desirable to ignore this reality and artificially pursue "socialism."

Latin America

The hot-spot of Latin America is Central America. Although both Nicaragua and El Salvador are now ruled by freely elected governments, civil conflicts and economic instability still convulse these countries; there has been unrest and turmoil in Panama followed by U.S. intervention to oust Colonel Manuel Noriega; and an anti-dictatorship struggle has been launched by the Haitian people.

Central America has become a tinderbox partly because of the intensification of contradictions among various political forces within several countries, and partly because of the heightened competition for influence in Central America between the two superpowers. The United States has long taken for granted that Latin America, and Central America in particular, is within its sphere of influence, and Washington is highly protective of its own "backyard." In order to maintain its control over Central America, the United States often pursues the policy of supporting one faction of a nation against another. For example, in Nicaragua the United States supplied Nicaraguan anti-government forces with large amounts of arms and economic aid in an attempt to overthrow the Sandinista government of Nicaragua. In El Salvador, on the other hand, the United States supports government forces in their struggle against the guerrillas. In Panama, U.S. policy is designed to keep a friendly government in power, so as to protect its interest in the Panama Canal. This approach led to the December 1989 invasion which succeeded in overthrowing Noriega, commander-in-chief of Panama's armed forces, under the banner of restoring democracy to Panama and ridding that country of a major narcotics trafficker. On the other hand, the Soviet Union has sought to establish its own zone of influence in the Caribbean by penetrating the region through Cuba and by providing direct military aid to Nicaragua.

The signing of a peace accord by the presidents of the five Central American nations in August 1987 has paved the way to a settlement of Central American issues. After the signing of the peace accord, the Nicaraguan government was the first to carry out a unilateral cease-fire and implemented an amnesty program, which moved the peace process forward in Central America. Another agreement was signed in February 1989 at the fourth summit meeting of Central American nations on the issues of repatriating more than 12,000 members of the Nicaraguan anti-government forces operating out of bases in Honduras and the acceleration of the democratization process in Nicaragua. Internationally supervised, free elections were held in April 1990 and brought to power a coalition of opposition political parties led by Violeta Chamorro.

The present situation is generally conducive to the peaceful settlement of Central American issues. The Central American people are weary of the chaos caused by war and eager for peace and stability. The Contadora and Lima groups, made up of some of the large nations of Latin America, are now cooperating with the UN Secretary General to promote the peace process in Central America. The Soviet Union has made clear that it has no interest in Central America and is willing to cooperate with the United States to settle all outstanding regional issues. Cuba has been behaving more cautiously than before. After coming to office, the Bush Administration declared that U.S. policy toward Central America is to seek settlement of disputes through diplomatic negotiations. But the peaceful settlement of Central American disputes is not all clear sailing. The two warring factions in El Salvador have not yet reached agreement, and it remains to be seen whether the Nicaraguan Contras and Sandinistas will abide by the results of the free elections. Whether the Bush Administration will further readjust U.S. policy toward Central America is crucial to a peaceful settlement of regional issues.

On the economic front, a grave international debt crisis shook the region in the early 1980s. Although this situation has been alleviated somewhat in recent years through debt negotiations and efforts by the involved nations, the issue is far from settled. The massive burden of debt has resulted in stagnation in production, steep reduction of foreign investment, and spiraling inflation in some Latin American countries. For instance, according to statistics compiled by the UN Economic Commission for Latin America, the inflation rate in 1988 in the region as a whole reached 470 percent while the economic growth rate is only 0.7 percent.[23] This explosive situation, if not attenuated, will trigger new crises that will be disruptive not only to the Latin American countries involved, but also to the creditor nations, of which the United States is the largest; and it will cause serious political turmoil as well as economic chaos. The worldwide debt crisis, which is most acute in Latin America, has become a grave international contradiction that has the potential to induce global financial and economic crisis, the danger of which should not be underestimated.

Although the debt crisis has its roots in the mistaken economic development strategies of some Latin American developing nations, the more fundamental cause lies in the consequences of developed countries endeavoring to extricate themselves from economic crises by exploiting the existing unfair and unreasonable international economic system and shifting economic troubles to Latin America and other developing countries. Latin American countries should readjust their developing strategies in the light of their own national conditions; in this respect, the experiences of some Asian nations are worth studying. At the same time, the Western developed countries should help debtor countries catch their breath by reducing and eliminating their debts and taking some concrete measures to improve North-South relations, to modify the unreasonable international economic order, to assist Latin American countries to adopt economic development programs that will provide steady if not spectacular growth, and to seek to resolve debt issues gradually by the benefits of sound economic development. In this respect, the proposal of March 1989 by American Secretary of the Treasury Nicholas Brady is a positive contribution. Under that proposal, support would be given to the joint efforts of the debtor countries and the commercial banks of the creditor countries to reduce the burden of interest repayments now facing the debtor nations. If this proposal can be implemented, it should go far to ease the international debt crisis.

---

[23] *People's Daily*, February 1, 1989.

Common Ground and Differences:
A Comparison of PRC and U.S. Third World Policies

In a comprehensive comparison and analysis of Chinese and U.S. policies toward various countries and regions in the third world, we can find much common ground and many similarities in their outlooks on the Asian-Pacific region. For instance, their policies are basically the same on Afghanistan, in parallel on other South Asian issues, and close to each other on Kampuchea. On Korea, the two countries adopt different positions: China supports North Korea whereas the United States backs South Korea, but both agree on the issue of maintaining peace and stability in the Korean Peninsula.

Toward the Middle East, Africa, and Central America, however, there exist significant differences between the Chinese and American positions. For instance, on the Middle East issue China strongly criticizes the United States for the latter's support for Israel and opposition to the PLO. On South Africa, China criticizes U.S. leaders for not putting enough pressure on South African authorities to end racial discrimination. On Central America, for a long time China had opposed American support of Nicaraguan anti-government forces and its flagrant interference in Nicaragua's internal affairs. On such issues as North-South relations and the establishment of the New International Economic Order,[24] the positions of China and the United States tend to be diametrically opposed.

There are a number of reasons why differences exist between China and the United States on their policies toward the third world. First, they have different points of departure. The United States is a superpower with global interests; its third world policies are based on the maintenance of its overseas interests. Belonging to the third world, China is now preoccupied with socialist modernization and needs a long-term, peaceful international environment conducive to its modernization program. What concerns China most is peace and stability in the Asian-Pacific region as well as throughout the world and establishment of good relations with its neighbors. Different points of departure will naturally lead to different policies. As a major third world country and a permanent member of the UN Security Council, China cannot but speak out and uphold justice on certain issues relating to third world countries.

---

[24]Developing countries have pressed for the establishment of a new international economic order to replace the old order which has been characterized by control of the world economy by the major economic powers. On May 1, 1974, a declaration establishing a new international economic order was passed by the Sixth Session of the United Nations General Assembly; it calls for every nation to have an equal right to participate in world economic activities, and for the developing countries to receive more favorable treatment in various fields of international economic cooperation.

Second, the United States is the leading industrial country whereas China is the largest developing one. The differences in their respective conditions and economic interests will certainly be reflected in their foreign policies.

Third, differences in social systems and ideologies will also be reflected in their policies toward the third world. What merits our attention here is that while China is emphasizing that state-to-state relations of peaceful coexistence transcend differences in social systems and ideologies, some Americans are stressing the role of ideology in international relations. American leaders are more apt to use their nation's power indiscreetly to influence internal affairs in third world countries. Applying American values, they try to use these weaker nations to serve America's interests. This is very harmful and naturally repugnant to China and other third world countries.

There are additional observations that should be mentioned in comparing the third world policies of China and the United States. First, despite the fact that China and the United States have policy differences over a number of issues related to the third world, these two countries have no direct conflict of interests over them. This is because China has no direct interests in the Middle East, Africa, and Central America; China's support to the Arab countries, the PLO, and the black people of South Africa, and so on, is largely moral, not material. The differences between China and the United States on these issues are reflected mainly in the debates at the United Nations and other international bodies—in other words, they are battles of words. Second, their differences in policies toward the third world, therefore, have not had much impact on U.S.-Chinese bilateral relations. What weakens these relations is not primarily differences in foreign policies, but U.S. interference with China's internal affairs on such issues as Taiwan. Third, in recent years the United States has either made some readjustments (for instance, on South African issues) or is prepared to do so (for instance, on Middle East and Central American issues). Meanwhile, China's own foreign policies, in their implementation, have become increasingly pragmatic and flexible. Consequently, Chinese and U.S. differences in this regard appear to be narrowing.

China pursues independent and peaceful foreign policies. Whether on international or domestic affairs, China will, as always, take positions and measures according to its own judgments and subject to no pressures from the superpowers or groups of big powers. China attaches great importance to Chinese-U.S. relations and holds that the stable development of such relations will not only benefit China and the United States, but also contribute significantly to the maintenance of peace and stability in the world. On third world issues, recognizing its disputes with the United States, China will continue to adhere to the principle of being independent and maintaining its own positions on the one hand, while also seeking common ground and attempting to resolve differences on the other hand, thus preventing these differences from adversely affecting bilateral relations.

China's Evolving Interests in the Western Pacific: Korea, Hong Kong, Taiwan, and ASEAN[1]

by Harlan W. Jencks

In the aftermath of the Beijing massacre of June 3-4, 1989, China's international relations are somewhat turbulent. The extent and duration of the damage, particularly with the democratic West, is not entirely clear. China's relations with the Korean states are relatively unchanged, but Beijing-Seoul diplomatic ties now seem to be inevitable. Relations with the Association of Southeast Asian States (ASEAN) are still affected by regional, rather than internal Chinese, developments. The already strained relationships with Hong Kong and the rival Republic of China (ROC) on Taiwan are considerably worse than before. Even more than usual, PRC foreign relations are not receiving the primary attention of national leaders. Internal issues of power and policy take precedence over virtually all foreign issues. As Robert Ross has recently shown, internal political turbulence does not usually correlate with radical departures in PRC foreign policy.[2] A caveat to that caveat is that Hong Kong and Taiwan are not exactly "foreign" issues. They are the subject matter of "reunification," an emotive national issue among senior PRC leaders.

In 1989, domestic developments complicated Chinese foreign policy just when the general situation in Asia was, otherwise, more promising than at any time since World War II. China, the Soviet Union, and the United States are all tending toward peaceful cooperative relationships. None is in a position to play the other two against each other. The foreign policies of all three are driven largely by internal, notably economic, imperatives. In all three countries, armed forces and military budgets are reduced from a few years ago.

---

[1] An earlier version of this paper was presented to the Conference on U.S.-PRC relations in the 1990s, sponsored by the Institute for East Asian Studies, University of California at Berkeley, and the Shanghai Institute of International Studies, at Ma'anshan, Anhui, PRC, May 15-18, 1989.

[2] Robert Ross, "From Lin Biao to Deng Xiaoping: Elite Instability and China's U.S Policy," *China Quarterly*, No. 118 (June 1989), pp. 296-299.

The alliance arrangements of both superpowers are deteriorating, and the international situation is increasingly multipolar. While the two superpowers are discussing mutual arms reductions and the prospects for global war appear to be quite low, regional powers are growing. Some long-standing regional disputes continue to be possible causes of war, so the Pacific area is not necessarily safer than it was ten or twenty years ago.[3] Closely related to the breakup of the bipolar world order, ideology is perhaps less important in international affairs than at any time since the Russian Revolution of 1917.[4]

The Superpowers

China assumed a truly equidistant position between the United States and the Soviet Union in 1989. Gorbachev's visit to Beijing in May 1989 warmed Beijing's relationship with the USSR only weeks before the Tiananmen massacre chilled relations with the United States. Gorbachev has been understanding and supportive of the Chinese crackdown, partly because he faces similar problems in trying to reform his economic and political systems without losing control.

The United States faces serious domestic economic and social problems. Abroad it faces the widespread perception, especially in Asia, that the United States is a world power in decline, overextended in its military and political commitments. Looming behind almost every American action or policy in Asia is our continuing balance of payments deficit.[5] Although the Asian security situation is more benign, ironically "this makes others less dependent on the United States, which . . . faces new challenges to find a convergence of interests with a generation of new leaders in Asia."[6]

For decades, a fundamental Soviet goal in Asia has been to be treated as a full-fledged member of the Pacific community. Brezhnev conducted a huge military buildup, crowned by acquisition of bases and an ally in Vietnam. Those are not achievements the Soviets will surrender lightly. Today the Russians push the "peace offensive" initiated by President Gorbachev in his Vladivostok speech of July 1986. His main achievement so far has been the Sino-Soviet detente.

---

[3]The following draws from Zhang Jingyi, "After the Superpowers," *Far East Economic Review* (cited hereafter as *FEER*), April 13, 1989, pp. 24-25.

[4]Ding Xinghao, "China's Policy in a Multi-Polar World," *Beijing Review*, Vol. 32, No.14 (April 3-9, 1989), p.14.

[5]U.S. Commerce Department, *Survey of Current Business*, Vol. 68, No. 3 (March 1988), pp. 42-43.

[6]Fred Greene, "The United States and Asia in 1988," *Asian Survey*, Vol. 29, No. 1 (January 1989), p.90.

Gorbachev essentially fulfilled the conditions China demanded for detente. He pulled Soviet forces out of Afghanistan and pressured Vietnam to withdraw from Cambodia. On April 5, 1989, the Vietnamese promised to withdraw their forces by September 30. The 1987 INF treaty with the United States led to dismantling SS-20 missiles in the Far East, which improved China's position in the correlation of forces. Gorbachev has made substantial troop reductions in Mongolia and the eastern part of the Soviet Union, and promised 200,000 more, as part of an overall 500,000-man reduction in the Soviet armed forces.[7] At the Beijing summit, he promised to deactivate eleven air regiments and sixteen warships in the Far East.

Sino-Soviet conflict has been a defining characteristic of the international scene for nearly thirty years. Thus, Sino-Soviet detente is the most important change in Asia since the Sino-American opening of 1970-1972. No one foresees restoration of the close military-strategic ties of the 1950s, and both sides are still suspicious of each other. For the foreseeable future, however, China and the Soviet Union have strong political and economic incentives to cooperate. Some 10,000 Chinese workers are at work on farms and in factories in the Soviet Far East. Cross-border trade and tourism are more active than at any time since 1960.[8]

In the aftermath of the Beijing massacre, expanded relations with the Soviet Union can, to some degree, compensate for the contraction of ties with the West. While the USSR is less advanced and less wealthy, PRC leaders may judge that, in compensation, Sino-Soviet ties will generate no by-product of "spiritual pollution." However, the Soviet Union is no longer the Stalinist prison Li Peng remembers from his student days in Moscow. Indeed, an "influx of Soviet specialists, teachers and students might exercise just as corrosive a cultural influence on China as did their Western counterparts in the 1980s." The experience of Russians, Hungarians, and Poles in the transition from Leninism toward democratic socialism is probably more relevant to China than the "abstract democratic values and political inexperience that most Westerners bring to China."[9]

Having "neutralized" China as a security threat, the Soviet Union has increased its efforts to undermine American power and presence,

[7]*Jane's Defence Weekly* (cited hereafter as *JDW*), March 25, 1989, p.523; and Tai Ming Cheung, "A Bad Year At Home But Better Abroad," *FEER*, March 2, 1989, p. 65.

[8]Gerald Segal, "The USSR in Asia in 1988," *Asian Survey*, Vol. 29, No. 1 (January 1989), pp. 102-103.

[9]Steven I. Levine, "The Uncertain Future of Chinese Foreign Policy," *Current History*, Vol. 88, No. 539 (September 1989), p.295.

especially military bases, in the western Pacific. Sino-Soviet detente contributes to the Soviet campaign against the American presence, by making the rest of Asia feel less dependent on the United States for security.[10]

On September 16, 1988, at Krasnoyarsk, Gorbachev proposed a Soviet-American "freeze" in naval and air deployments in the Pacific and offered not to increase nuclear weapons there if the United States would not deploy new ones.[11] The Soviets recognize that such arms control proposals can disrupt U.S. relations with friends and allies, even if the proposals have little chance of being accepted or implemented. Indeed, some are never formally proposed in diplomatic channels at all, their sole purpose being to embarrass the United States.

The effect of the Soviet force reductions announced in Beijing remains to be seen. Much depends on the specific forces withdrawn. For example, 16 old *Romeo* and *Whiskey* class submarines could be deactivated with a net *gain* for the efficiency, economy, and safety of the Soviet Pacific Fleet (SOVPACFLT). Assuming that at least some modern forces are withdrawn, there will be a significant reduction in Soviet *anti-Chinese* military power. Moscow will try to use those reductions to press for U.S. and Japanese military reductions, even though the cutbacks may not affect Soviet capabilities against the United States and Japan at all.

Notwithstanding the recent reductions, Soviet military power in East Asia has increased enormously over the past decade. SOVPACFLT has added at least 40 major vessels, growing from the smallest to the largest of the four Soviet fleets. Moscow recently began deploying SS-25 mobile intercontinental ballistic missiles in Asia. They can cover all targets formerly covered by the SS-20s. Gorbachev's freeze would preserve the relative increase of Soviet Far Eastern military power.

Tbilisi, the first Soviet conventional aircraft carrier, is expected to be commissioned in the near future, followed by the second of her class in 1991 or 1992. A newer class of about 75,000 tons (the size of a U.S. *Nimitz*-class carrier) was laid down in November 1988 in a Black Sea shipyard.[12] It is reasonable to expect that these carriers are intended for the SOVPACFLT, and it is reasonable to wonder how they will be used. A recent Soviet book on naval doctrine emphasizes the strategic strike

---

[10]Greene, op. cit., p. 90.

[11]Moscow Radio, September 16, 1988; translated in Foreign Broadcast Information Service, *Soviet Union*, 1988, No. 181.

[12]*JDW*, March 29, 1989, pp. 495, 524.

role of the aircraft carrier, pointing out that the trend in strategic-level warfare is "expansion of the scope of these military operations, the further increase in the importance of the surprise factor, [and] the expansion of the sphere of strategic missions carried out in maritime and oceanic TVDs [Theaters of Military Operations]."[13]

That does not sound "defensive." Yet the whole centerpiece of the Soviet "peace offensive" has been the alleged adoption of a "defensive" strategy of "military sufficiency." Overall, however, *perestroika* and *glasnost* have led to less visibly aggressive Soviet international behavior. The SOVPACFLT has had fewer out-of-area maneuvers since 1988, and its few large-scale maneuvers seem to have been intended to "protect land-based assets."[14]

Personalities and Domestic Politics

Domestic politics influence the foreign relations of all states. A disturbing aspect of the international situation in the Far East, however, is that so much depends upon two individuals: Deng Xiaoping and Mikhail Gorbachev. Gorbachev is young and vigorous, but he has many political enemies. Opponents of *perestroika* are ready to seize upon the inevitable problems of reform to turn back the clock, as they did in China in June 1989. In addition to "democracy movements," reform and opening have unleashed repressed nationalism in both countries (Lithuania, Armenia, Tibet, et al.). Deng is nearing the end of his active political life, and appears politically vulnerable for the first time in a decade, as a result of the dramatic events of spring 1989. In suppressing the "democracy movement" he allied himself with the nominally "retired" party elders. These "proletarian revolutionaries of the older generation" have generally opposed his domestic reform policies, and some (e.g., Wang Zhen) oppose opening to the outside world as well. The elders are now trying to restrict Deng's power. There are even graver uncertainties regarding a future without him.

Mongolia

Gorbachev's most impressive military concessions involve Mongolia, which Mao Zedong once described as "a fist in China's back." For decades, the Soviet 39th Combined Arms Army in Mongolia has been positioned to strike southeast toward Beijing along the shortest route. In

---

[13]*The Fleet: Roles, Perspective for Development, Employment* (Moscow, 1988); quoted in *JDW*, March 29, 1989, p.524.

[14]*JDW*, March 25, 1989, p. 496.

January 1987, Gorbachev withdrew one motorized rifle division. In March 1989, he announced withdrawal of all Soviet air forces and all but one of the remaining divisions.[15] In addition, the Mongolian government announced on March 3 that it would reduce its armed forces from 25,000 to 13,000 soldiers, deactivating two of its four motor rifle divisions and 18 aircraft. It will also demobilize some 200,000 reservists and cut its defense budget by about 11 percent.[16] Sino-Mongolian relations are the closest in twenty-five years. A number of joint economic ventures are under way, and thousands of Chinese workers are now in Mongolia.

Korea

In the 1950s, Beijing supported the Democratic People's Republic of Korea (DPRK) for ideological reasons, and as a buffer against "American imperialism." In the 1960s and 1970s, however, policy toward Pyongyang became little more than a facet of the Sino-Soviet conflict. Kim Il Sung skillfully played his giant neighbors against each other, receiving economic and military aid from both. Since 1961, the DPRK has had the remarkable distinction of maintaining active mutual defense treaties with both. Moscow and Beijing, while paying lip-service to Kim's reunification demands, provided only moderate levels of military assistance, and quietly restrained his more aggressive adventures. Like the United States and Japan, they made it clear that they wanted the peninsula to remain peaceful, even if that meant remaining divided.[17]

The emergence of the Republic of Korea (ROK) as a world trading power, the Sino-Soviet detente, and Seoul's restiveness with its American patron broke the status quo in the mid-1980s. In 1983, Seoul and Beijing negotiated directly for the return to China of a high-jacked airliner. Soon after, China publicly admitted its indirect trade with the ROK, and stopped pretending to suppress it.

Friendly Sino-American relations facilitated rapid development of PRC-ROK trade, which rose from about US$1.5 billion in 1987 to perhaps US$3 billion in 1988.[18] China has become a major source of food and

---

[15]*JDW*, April 1, 1989, p. 544.

[16]*JDW*, March 18, 1989, p. 447; and *FEER*, March 23, 1989, p. 9.

[17]Edward A. Olsen, "Does anyone really want Korean reunification?," *Asian Wall Street Journal*, May 16, 1983.

[18]Because much of this trade still flows through third parties, statistics are not too reliable. Ken Yun, "Crossing the Yellow Sea," *China Business Review*, January-February 1989, p. 39. This discussion draws heavily on Soohyun Chon, "Korea's Role as a Developing Economy: Its Trade Relationship with the United States and China," Paper presented to the IEAS-SIIS Conference on U.S. and PRC Security Policy in Asia, May 15-18, 1989, Ma'anshan, Anhui, PRC.

coal for South Korea, while ROK businessmen have set up joint enterprises utilizing China's relatively cheap labor.[19] Increasingly complex trade arrangements require legal and diplomatic protection, so both countries have opened quasi-diplomatic representative offices, despite Pyongyang's outrage. Many observers expect formal Beijing-Seoul relations will be established within the next year or two.

Perhaps the cooling in PRC-DPRK relations seemed to offer an opening to Moscow. In the spring of 1984, shortly after Washington agreed to sell F-16 fighter planes to the ROK, the Soviet Union announced it would provide MiG-23 fighters to North Korea. Since then, Soviet military aid has included SA-3 and SA-5 air defense missiles, Su-25 attack planes, and MiG-29 fighters.[20] This development is disturbing, particularly because the Russians resisted North Korean requests for military aid throughout the Brezhnev era. Despite the military advantages and increased influence in Pyongyang, Soviet arms transfers seem at variance with Gorbachev's peace offensive.

Increased Soviet influence in Pyongyang is not necessarily a bad thing; the Russians, after all, have a stake in restraining North Korean adventurism. Nevertheless, Moscow has introduced much-improved military technology into North Korea. The Russians gained access to DPRK airspace and facilities to the detriment of China and the United States. Since 1985, Soviet aircraft have flown across North Korea or their way to collect electronic intelligence against China and U.S. bases in the Philippines. Recently, Soviet Tu-16 bombers reportedly have refueled in North Korea on their way to Vietnam.[21]

The North Koreans are clearly unhappy about the warmer Sino-Soviet relationship, and are in a dilemma about opening to the outside world. The tide of reform in Vietnam, China, the Soviet Union, and Eastern Europe will eventually force them to follow suit. Pyongyang is also under international pressure because of the economic and diplomatic success of the ROK. Hungary opened diplomatic relations with Seoul in mid-1989, and other East Europeans have followed suit. In 1988, the USSR sent business representatives to Seoul along with its Olympic athletes. Soviet-ROK trade is growing, and there is talk of semi-official representation.

China, the USSR, the ROK, and the United States all seem to agree that North Korean isolation needs to end. At the urging of ROK President

---

[19]Soohyun Chon, op. cit., pp. 16-17.

[20]Tai Ming Cheung, "The Doctrine of minimal defense unfolds slowly," *FEER*, February 9, 1989, p. 28; and Daniel Abele, "Soviet-North Korean Relations on the Upswing," *Radio Liberty Research*, August 24, 1987, p. 3.

[21]"Tu-16 Badgers Refuel in North Korea," *JDW*, February 11, 1989, p.204.

Roh Tae Woo, informal American contacts with North Korea expanded in 1988-1989.[22] The principal DPRK demand for improved relations is complete withdrawal of American forces from the south. The principal American demand is "credible assurances" that North Korea has abandoned state terrorism.[23] Neither demand is likely to be met soon.

As long as North Korea has a penchant for violent irresponsible actions, it is good for everybody else in Asia that the Sino-Soviet detente has robbed Kim of his ability to play China and the Soviet Union against each other. China and the Soviet Union deserve credit for restraining North Korean terrorism during the 1988 Olympiad. Nevertheless, Pyongyang remains dangerously unpredictable, the more so because of the succession crisis which is almost certain to follow the impending death of Kim Il Sung.

There have been a few encouraging developments in intra-Korean relations.[24] Nearly all Koreans genuinely want reunification, which would remove a chronic threat to peace. It is probably best for outsiders to stay out of the reunification process. The PRC, Soviet Union, and the United States should avoid complicating the situation by escalating military aid, sales, or commitments.

The United States and the ROK need to revise their military relationship. South Korea is capable of defending itself until American reinforcements arrive. Continued U.S. dominance of Combined Forces Command (CFC) cannot be justified militarily. The United States' adverse trade balance is a further incentive to reduce forces drastically in Korea. A substantial American troop withdrawal would also make it much easier for China to improve its relationship with the ROK, and would reduce an impediment to Korean reunification.[25]

Taipei, Seoul, and Beijing

The ROK and the ROC have been close friends for decades. Each has a special relationship with the United States, is staunchly anti-communist, and is in competition with a rival national communist regime. In the 1980s, however, their diplomatic fortunes diverged. Seoul won increased recognition at the expense of Pyongyang, while Taipei[26] lost recognition in favor of Beijing. As noted above, Sino-Soviet detente has

---

[22]*New York Times*, November 1, 1988.

[23]Greene, op. cit., p. 97.

[24]John McBeth, *FEER*, March 2, 1989, pp. 22-23.

[25]*New York Times*, July 18, 1988: and McBeth, op. cit., pp. 21-22.

[26]The ROC capital is spelled "Taipei" on Taiwan, and "Taibei" on the mainland.

contributed to increased Russian and PRC trade with Seoul. That, plus decreased North Korean influence, may eventually lead to "cross recognition" of South Korea by Beijing and Moscow. That would mean for Taipei a loss of recognition by Seoul, which would be a major diplomatic setback (and a major incentive for Beijing to establish diplomatic relations with Seoul).

Were Seoul to recognize Beijing, the cooperation between Taiwanese and South Korean military industries would also be at risk. The ROK is a convenient channel through which American arms and technology can reach Taiwan. Additionally, the two countries can achieve economies of scale with military co-production deals. A controversial current example is the proposed purchase by Taipei of 16 *Ulsan* class frigates. Some Taiwan legislators believe the deal should be canceled in favor of more costly but secure production of a Taiwan design in Taiwan. Their argument for self-sufficiency is partly based on the possibility that Seoul is poised to desert the ROC.

Taiwan

The Sino-Soviet detente is a mixed blessing for Taiwan. If Beijing were to decide to use force to "reunify the fatherland" it would be less constrained by the need to defend its northern border. On the other hand, the "China card" is less useful to the United States than ever, so Washington may feel less compelled to consider PRC wishes with respect to Taiwan policy.[27] Moreover, sympathy for Taiwan in the U.S. Congress has been reinforced by revulsion against the Beijing massacre and subsequent repression.

Both rival Chinese governments, for their own reasons, encourage trade and human contact across the Taiwan Strait. Since 1986, Taipei's so-called "Three Nos" policy (no negotiations, no contact, no compromise with the "communist rebels") has been interpreted ever more flexibly. There are several interrelated reasons for this. First, the Kuomintang (KMT) leadership is trying to preserve a sense of being *Chinese* among its people by renewing personal and family contacts with the mainland. Beijing shares that desire, and has facilitated trade and travel, hoping it will contribute to peaceful reunification. Another reason is the increasing clout of the Taiwan business community, which wants to take advantage of linguistic, cultural, and family affinities to get in on the PRC's "opening to the world."[28]

---

[27]Lina Hsu, "Political Scientists Analyze Summit," *Free China Journal* (cited hereafter as *FCJ*), May 25, 1989, p. 2.

[28]Lucian W. Pye, "Taiwan's Development and Its Implications for Beijing and Washington," *Asian Survey*, Vol. 26, No. 6 (June 1986), pp. 611-629.

Up to June 1989, direct and indirect trade between Taiwan and the mainland was growing rapidly. In 1988 it was about US$2.7 billion, some 66 percent over 1987. Added to that was about US$3 billion spent by Taiwan visitors to the mainland. Taiwan investment in the PRC is estimated at about US$400 million.[29]

That much trade is bound to have political ramifications. Both sides have tried to use "people's diplomacy" to convince the other's population that the system across the strait is better. Taiwan has been the winner in this competition on virtually all fronts. Beijing could have tolerated that if Taiwan exhibited only a superior living standard. Instead, Taiwan has pursued a conscious effort to "undercut communism"[30] by exporting what might be called "bourgeois liberalism with Chinese characteristics." The day after the Tiananmen massacre, while the rest of the world was cutting itself off from the PRC in protest, the ROC government lifted its prohibition against direct telephone and mail links with the mainland. ROC President Lee Teng-hui's first reaction to the news was reportedly, "We not only shouldn't stop the family reunion visits, we should expand them."[31]

KMT leaders have learned first hand that the momentum created by free market economics and foreign trade is accompanied by social and political reform. Conservatives may try to retain a Leninist polity beside a market economy, but it cannot be done. The economic market implies and creates a political market. The process is fed by modern business with its international travel, direct-dial telephones, and fax machines.

Owing to forty years of communist propaganda, the KMT party is still thoroughly discredited on the mainland, despite the well-known Taiwan success story. For instance, in July 1989, exiled student leader Wu'er Kaixi stalked out of a Chicago meeting with Cheng Hsin-hsiung when he learned that the latter was Chairman of the KMT's Overseas Affairs Committee.[32]

On the diplomatic front, the PRC has been trying to force Taiwan out of international organizations and into isolation. Over 150 governments recognize the Beijing government, while only 24 recognize Taipei. However, Taiwan is such an important economic and trading power that it cannot be ignored. Taipei is skillfully using its economic clout to gain

---

[29]Tai Ming Cheung, *FEER*, March 2, 1989, p. 66.

[30]"War of Ideas Said ROC Strategy," *FCJ*, August 7, 1989, p.1.

[31]"Premier Keeps Door Open," *FCJ*, June 8, 1989, p. 3.

[32]*FEER*, August 10, 1989, p.8.

and maintain friends and retain its memberships. It has semi-official representation in many countries, and recently began trade talks in Eastern Europe, Vietnam, and even the Soviet Union.

Within organizations as diverse as the Asian Development Bank (ADB) and the International Olympic Committee, Taiwan and Beijing tolerate each other's presence, often contesting the arcane issue of the name used to designate Taipei's representatives. Beijing currently insists that its rival be called "Taibei, China (*Taibei, Zhongguo*)" which connotes Taiwan's subordination to Beijing. Taipei would prefer to be "China" but has compromised on "Chinese, Taiwan (*Zhonghua Taiwan*)" which connotes distinct status.[33]

In order to participate in international organizations, Taiwan sports teams and delegations have been traveling to the mainland for several years, each accompanied by a volley of statements that its activities in no way constitute any reversal of the "Three Nos" policy. The most spectacular example so far was the attendance of ROC Finance Minister Shirley Kuo at the ADB meeting in Beijing on May 4-6, 1989.[34] Taiwan is aggressively pursuing entry or reentry into economic organizations like GATT and OECD, and ultimately hopes somehow to reenter the UN.[35]

Faced with progressive diplomatic isolation in late 1988, Taipei undertook a new "flexible policy." It will no longer automatically sever diplomatic ties with a government that extends recognition to Beijing. It is now up to that government to sever ties. Thus, the PRC must insist upon excluding ROC diplomats from smaller states that want to retain economic ties with Taiwan. With the notable exceptions of the ROK and Saudi Arabia, most of the governments still recognizing Taipei are small and poor, a fact Taipei is successfully exploiting with generous aid programs. It recently established a ROC International Economic Cooperation Development Fund of US$1.2 billion to "assist nations friendly to the ROC through investment or technology transfer."[36]

The ROC gained recognition from the Bahamas in January 1989.[37] A turning point may have been reached on July 21, when Grenada, which

---

[33]"No More Name Changing," *FCJ*, January 30, 1989, p.1.

[34]Osman Tseng, "Pragmatic and Flexible," *Free China Review*, Vol.39, No. 7 (July 1989), pp. 63-65.

[35]"ROC Takes Aim At Old UN Seat," *FCJ*, April 13, 1989, p.1; and "'Little Dragons' Meet OECD," *FCJ*, January 30, 1989, p. 8.

[36]*FCJ*, August 17, 1989, p.2.

[37]*FCJ*, January 23, 1989, p. 1.

already had diplomatic ties with Beijing, extended diplomatic recognition to Taipei, becoming the first government to recognize both. Beijing protested, but did not withdraw its representatives until early August. This was the first PRC loss of recognition to Taiwan. Liberia and Lesotho followed in late 1989. Taipei is actively encouraging other countries to follow the "Grenada model."[38]

The United States recognized the PRC in the 1970s for strategic reasons which still apply to the United States and other major powers. However, most of the smaller states that followed suit and shifted recognition to Beijing did so for economic reasons. The mesmerizing myth of the "vast China market" kept foreign businessmen agitating their governments for diplomatic recognition of Beijing throughout the 1980s. But the "China market" has proven frustrating and unprofitable for most businessmen, while Taiwan continues to be a safe, profitable, and congenial place to do business. The Beijing massacre reversed the liberalizing trend on the mainland, making it still harder to do business there, and stripped away some of its mystique. Taiwan looks still better by comparison.

Small poor countries, especially those outside Asia, have little practical reason to stick with Beijing, and may be contemplating the "Grenada model." Grenada had formal diplomatic relations with both Chinas for eleven days. Behind the scenes, no doubt, PRC diplomats were using every tool at their disposal to persuade Grenada to reverse its decision. That alone was tacit recognition that the Grenadans had every reason to go with Taipei if forced to choose, and that other small states might well follow suit. With its "flexible policy," plus Beijing's bloody new image, Taipei may have turned or at least stemmed the diplomatic tide.

The ROC Foreign Ministry disingenuously "indicated that the establishment of diplomatic ties with Grenada does not, in any way, construe [sic] Taipei's move towards a 'dual-recognition' or a 'two-China' policy."[39] Yet Taipei has floated the slogan "one nation, two governments" in contrast to Beijing's "One country, two systems." Clearly, President Lee is trying to create a legitimate international political position for Taiwan. Whether he is trying to get recognition as a separate Chinese state is not clear. Mainland observers are certain that the "flexible policy" is leading toward a de facto "Two Chinas" policy.[40]

Taipei would assume great risks if it actually did pursue a "One China,

---

[38]"Grenada A Turning Point?," *FCJ*, July 27, 1989, p.4.

[39]Ibid.

[40]This discussion draws heavily on a conference discussion held in Ma'anshan, Anhui, on May 15, 1989.

One Taiwan" or a "Two Chinas" policy. The PRC has declared that it would invade the island if it declared independence. Perhaps more important is the internal legitimacy of the KMT-dominated Republic of China government, whose right to rule is based on the principle that there is only one China, of which Taipei is the legal "temporary" capital. Advocacy of Taiwan independence is the one political crime that still can get one jailed in Taiwan.

But times are changing. The KMT has struck deep roots, and true parliamentary democracy is emerging. President Lee is a native Taiwanese, and the image of the KMT as a pack of mainland carpetbaggers is fading.[41] The next generation of KMT leaders will not need the myth of being the government of all China.

The Taiwan Relations Act of 1979 commits the United States "to maintain the capacity . . . to resist any resort to force or other forms of coercion that would jeopardize the security, or the social or economic system, of the people on Taiwan." Taiwan is still a far more important and mutually profitable trading partner than the mainland, even after nearly twenty years of U.S.-PRC trade. More importantly, Americans just do not want to see Taiwan reunified with the mainland by force. Recent improvements in human rights and democratization in Taiwan, in stark contrast to the mainland situation, have strengthened the commitment.

Beijing recognizes that the American commitment to Taiwan is "a question left over by history." However, since it was American intervention in 1950-1954 that divided China in the first place,[42] and since American arms have perpetuated the division, Beijing finds it hypocritical for Americans to say that we do not want to intervene in the reunification process. China's leaders want Washington to pressure Taipei into accepting Beijing's terms. The United States would have much to lose and nothing to gain by that, however. No one really seems to expect the situation to change.

The current situation is legally ambiguous, but the Chinese have a genius for living with ambiguity. Because Americans cannot tolerate ambiguity, we continue to anchor our Taiwan policy on the legalistic myth (rejected by both Taipei and Beijing) that the status of Taiwan is "unsettled."[43]

---

[41]Pye, op. cit.

[42]For a landmark analysis of American policy toward Taiwan in the 1950s, see Joseph H. deRivera, *The Psychological Dimension of Foreign Policy* (Columbus, OH: Merrill, 1966).

[43]In a letter to UN Secretary General Trygvie Lie on August 25, 1950, President Truman, justifying American intervention in the Taiwan Strait the previous June, declared: "The actual status of the island is that it is territory taken from Japan by the victory of the Allied Forces in the Pacific. Like other such territories, its legal status cannot be fixed until there

American policy toward Taiwan has been consistent since the U.S.-PRC joint communique of August 1982, particularly regarding the transfer of military technology. Military sales to Taiwan in fiscal year 1988 totaled US$700 million, of which US$505 million was under the Foreign Military Sales (FMS) program and US$195 million was under the Arms Export Act. The Bush Administration requested US$660 million (US$475 million FMS and US$185 million commercial) in arms sales to Taiwan for fiscal 1990. That would be US$20 million less than in fiscal 1989, a gradual reduction in line with the 1982 communique.[44]

PRC observers, and some Americans, still believe Washington can dictate to Taipei. In fact, Taiwan is now a major economic power, the world's 13th largest trader in 1988. Taipei has friends and options all over the world. As suggested above, their diplomatic fortunes may be changing as well. If the United States were to pressure Taiwan to compromise with the PRC (which is unlikely), Taiwan might exercise options less desirable for the United States and for the PRC. To name only one, Taiwan is quite capable of developing nuclear weapons very quickly, if it ever feels sufficiently threatened.

In the aftermath of the Beijing tragedy in June 1989, Washington may want to readjust its Taiwan policy. While the United States must maintain formal diplomatic relations with the PRC, now is an ideal time to strengthen quasi-official ties with Taiwan. On June 7, 1989, in a nicely timed move, the Bush Administration announced a US$108 million sale of military parts and equipment to Taipei. The administration might consider increasing quotas for ROC military officers at American service schools, perhaps allowing them to wear their uniforms here. Such symbolic action would not really be threatening to Beijing, but it would strengthen Taiwan diplomatically, while signaling our moral outrage over further political repression on the mainland.

Meanwhile, the ROC continues to strengthen its defenses, especially air and sea forces. Construction of the first eight *Kwang Hua I* class frigates (a modification of the American *Oliver Hazard Perry* class) began in January 1990, with assistance from Bath Iron Works. The indigenously

---

is international action to determine its future. The [ROC] Chinese Government was asked by the Allies to take the surrender of the Japanese forces on the island. That is the reason the Chinese are there now."

This remains the American legal position. In the Shanghai Communique of February 27, 1972, "The U.S. side declared: The United States acknowledges that all Chinese on either side of the Taiwan Strait maintain there is but one China and that Taiwan is a part of China. The United States Government does not challenge that position." Similar language in subsequent statements has maintained the legal fig-leaf.

[44]"U.S. Arms Sales Drop," *FCJ*, February 2, 1989, p. 1.

designed AT-3 jet trainer/attack aircraft is now in production. In May 1989, the "Ching-kuo" fighter made its first test flight.[45] Over the past decade, the ROC military has diversified its sources of arms. The new ships are equipped with a mix of U.S. and West European weapons systems.[46]

The fate of Hong Kong will largely determine whether a new generation of leaders in Taiwan decides to declare independence, pursue peaceful reunification, or maintain the ambiguous status quo. If the Sino-British Joint Agreement of 1984 is faithfully implemented, and Hong Kong does in fact become a "special economic zone with a highly autonomous economic and social system," then there is reason to hope for peaceful Taiwan-mainland reunification fairly early in the next century. If Hong Kong is not allowed to remain highly autonomous, if the legal system and the human rights situation in Hong Kong become noticeably worse, it is quite possible that Taiwan leaders who have no living memory of the mainland may decide to establish formally a separate Chinese state on their island.

There are disturbing possibilities. Faced with Taiwan's increasing prosperity and diplomatic resurgence, and with the long-term possibility of Taiwan independence, the old men in Beijing may reverse their peaceful reunification policy of the past decade. Threat, blockade, or even attempted invasion cannot be ruled out, although military action is unlikely until after 1997.

Hong Kong

Taiwan's future depends upon Hong Kong's fate, which in turn depends upon the PRC's internal political evolution between now and 1997. Beijing has powerful economic and diplomatic incentives to leave Hong Kong alone after taking over from Britain—to honor its commitment under the 1984 Joint Declaration to leave the internal social and economic system unchanged for fifty years. Well over half of PRC foreign trade flows through Hong Kong. The city is the world's third leading financial center and one of its busiest ports.

But the "proletarian revolutionaries of the older generation" now running the PRC believe they have overriding political reasons for doing to Hong Kong what they are currently doing to the mainland. Hong Kong has been a major source of the "bourgeois liberal" contagion sweeping

---

[45]*FCJ*, June 1, 1989, p. 1.

[46]*JDW*, April 11, 1989, p. 539.

through China in the late 1980s. Today it is a scene of continued protest and support for the fugitive victims of repression. Beijing has made no secret of its desire to crush dissent in Hong Kong. If that means throwing out the economic "baby" with the political "bath water," then the old men in Beijing are quite prepared to do so.

The Basic Law for the "Hong Kong Special Autonomous Region" promulgated in March 1990 fell far short of the specific guarantees of personal political rights Hong Kong has had under British law.[47] Communist authorities retain the prerogative to intervene against any political activity of which they disapprove. Already, they are flagrantly violating their 1984 pledge not to interfere in Hong Kong's internal affairs before 1997. In July 1989, for instance, a coalition of Hong Kong Chinese organized the Hong Kong Alliance in Support of the Patriotic Democratic Movement. *People's Daily* responded with a vicious attack, accusing the Hong Kong government of "turning a blind eye to the . . . Alliance . . . whose plan was to turn the territory into a 'base for overthrowing the Chinese government.'"[48] PRC intervention to suppress dissent, before 1997, and in violation of the 1984 Agreement, is likely unless Britain and the other democracies act to prevent it.

There are plenty of villains in the Hong Kong situation. Great Britain just wants to withdraw in 1997, without any unseemly fuss and with British investments safe. London steadfastly refuses to consider granting right of abode in Britain to any but an elite few Hong Kong residents.[49] The people of the UK simply will not tolerate the possibility of an influx of 5.5 million Hong Kong Chinese. No British politician can advocate free immigration and hope to be reelected, so none does. Instead, Britain issues bland assurances that everything will be fine.

The Western democracies are more interested in protecting their investments than in helping Hong Kong's people. In fact, up to June 1989, Japanese and American investment was flowing into Hong Kong faster than Hong Kong capital was fleeing. It is too soon to be sure, but that will probably not change.

The people of Hong Kong are almost exclusively concerned with their own families and the safety of personal assets. Everyone who can afford it is sending liquid assets and family members overseas to establish safe haven. Only a courageous few are fighting for democratic reforms and

---

[47]"Basic Law of HKSAR [Hong Kong Special Autonomous Region], PRC," *China Daily*, April 5, 1990, p .3.

[48]*South China Morning Post*, July 22, 1989, pp. 1,5; in FBIS, *China*, 1989, No. 140, p. 88.

[49]In contrast, Lisbon has granted right of abode in Portugal to Macao's people. Ironically, under EC agreements they will then be free to immigrate to Britain.

legal guarantees. Their battle appears quixotic. The brain-drain is already a major factor in the labor market, and promises to worsen. As morale and technical competence continue to fall in the civil service and police, civil unrest seems inevitable.[50] Hong Kong Chinese mistreatment of Vietnamese refugees is blatantly racist.[51]

After 1997, Hong Kong will retain little of its professional and middle class. It will have neither the free press nor the legal basis for continued commercial and financial prominence. At best, it will be a particularly prosperous PRC city, with a large expatriate community manning its severely contracted commercial, financial, and manufacturing sector. Its population will consist of communist cadres, local "patriotic" businessmen (with substantial foreign bank accounts), and a resentful population of unskilled and semi-skilled Chinese who were unable to escape. At worst, by 1997, Hong Kong may simply be the world's largest refugee camp.

Southeast Asia

Ironically, the Socialist Republic of Vietnam (SRV) has been the most vocal foreign supporter of the Tiananmen massacre. Like China and the USSR, the Vietnamese are trying to reform. PRC confrontation with Vietnam, while still serious, is at the lowest point in a decade, because of the Sino-Soviet detente and progress on the Cambodian issue, more than because of their shared reform problems.

Since Vietnam invaded Cambodia in December 1978, China, the United States, and the Association of Southeast Asian Nations (ASEAN) have generally agreed that the SRV is the principal security problem in the region. The Sino-Vietnamese conflict over Cambodia, especially China's incursion into Vietnam in early 1979, helped cement a military relationship between Vietnam and the Soviet Union. That relationship led to establishment of Soviet military facilities at Cam Ranh Bay and Da Nang, which deeply concern the United States and ASEAN.

In his Krasnoyarsk speech of September 1988, President Gorbachev offered to "trade" Soviet withdrawal from Vietnamese bases for American withdrawal from Philippine bases. Although the Vietnamese regard the Soviet bases as a guarantee against Chinese attack, they are proud people who dislike having foreign forces on their soil. They resent the Soviets' offer of the bases as "bargaining chips." The PRC and all of the

---

[50]Emily Lau, "Chinese top cop," *FEER*, August 17, 1989, pp. 26-27.

[51]*FEER*, August 17, 1989, pp. 29-31.

ASEAN governments have expressed, at least informally, their desire for the U.S. military to remain in Southeast Asia, but none is willing to host permanent American bases.

On February 23, 1989, in Tokyo, China and Indonesia announced they would normalize diplomatic relations. Although neither side seemed to be in any hurry, the Beijing massacre apparently did not slow the process. Normalization talks were held in September 1989 at the United Nations, and they reached a successful conclusion in August 1990. PRC diplomatic ties with Indonesia will also allow Singapore to open formal ties with China, so the PRC will finally have formal relations with every country in the region.[52]

Fear and suspicion of China are widespread in Southeast Asia, having deep historical roots. PRC relations in the region may be better than they have been in decades, but traditional anti-Chinese sentiment remains. Even China's 1987-1989 sales of military equipment to Thailand have provoked concern in Indonesia and Malaysia. The ASEAN governments are uncomfortable with close Sino-American ties, not only because they fear China, but because they see themselves in competition with the PRC for U.S. support, markets, and investment. The June 1989 cooling of American relations with China was therefore quietly welcomed in the region. On the other hand, the United States is in a position to mediate between China and ASEAN, if and when it decides to do so.[53]

Until recently, the Cambodian situation appeared to be stuck in an endless blood-letting. Recent initiatives by Prince Norodom Sihanouk, Thailand, Indonesia, Australia, and the UN, and the Sino-Soviet detente, led to some progress toward a settlement. In July 1987, China announced that it was opposed to the Khmer Rouge returning to exclusive power. In 1988 China went even further by offering to cut supplies to the Cambodian resistance in tandem with a "complete" withdrawal of Vietnamese troops and advisors from Cambodia. China began to show flexibility on the role of the Khmer Rouge in a settlement and even stated, in July 1988, that some "unacceptable" persons should be barred from any new government. After refusing to discuss the Cambodian question with China for many years, the Soviets took up the issue with China in August 1988 and reached a broad agreement, leading to Foreign Minister Qian Qichen's visit to Moscow in December

---

[52]*FEER*, March 9, 1989, pp. 10-11.

[53]I am grateful to Professor Ji Guoxing of the Shanghai Institute of International Studies (SIIS) for sharing his views.

1988, Foreign Minister Shevardnadze's visit to Beijing in February 1989, and the Deng-Gorbachev summit in Beijing in May.[54]

The Vietnamese announcement in March 1989 that they would withdraw their remaining troops from Cambodia by September 30 put urgent pressure on all parties to devise a workable political solution. China and the Soviet Union both made important concessions during Foreign Minister Shevardnadze's visit. They accepted, in principle, an "effective international control mechanism" to oversee a Cambodian settlement. However, crucial details remain to be settled. The "mechanism" will have to be a moderately large and well-armed force if it is to "exercise strict supervision over Vietnamese withdrawal, cessation of foreign military aid, maintenance of peace, and the conduct of free elections."[55] The onus is on the resistance forces of the Coalition Government of Democratic Kampuchea (CGDK) and on the Vietnamese-sponsored Khmer People's Republic (KPR) to devise a solution to the "knotty basic issue" of Cambodia's future governance and how it is to be achieved. What is needed is a

> new governing structure . . . that: (1) is acceptable to all of the major contending Khmer factions; (2) meets Hanoi's legitimate national security interest that a hostile regime not come to power in Phnom Penh; (3) permits the Chinese the degree of presence/influence/status that they feel is their due; (4) is acceptable to ASEAN (particularly Thailand in terms of its security needs); and (5) major outsiders, the USSR, U.S. and Japan, can live with (a lesser problem).[56]

Talk about "free elections" in Cambodia is mere posturing. Cambodian reality—the lack of any democratic tradition, to say nothing of 30-40,000 well-armed Khmer Rouge troops—makes the holding of "free elections" impossible. If a solution is found, it will involve the use and/or the balancing of force.

After the failure of the International Conference on Cambodia in Paris (July 30-August 30, 1989), the Vietnamese "withdrew" on September 30, 1989, leaving behind advisors and some Vietnamese soldiers in KPR uniforms. Fighting intensified briefly, until more Vietnamese troops returned to stabilize the situation.[57] Further diplomatic progress awaits a

---

[54]Nayan Chanda, *FEER*, March 23, 1989, p. 10; and Tai Ming Cheung, *FEER*, March 2, 1989, p. 65.

[55]Robert Delfs, "A United Front Again," *FEER*, March 30, 1989, p. 27.

[56]Douglas Pike, *Indochina Chronicle*, Vol. 7, No. 3 (July-Sept. 1988), p. 11.

[57]"PAVN troops in Cambodia," *JDW*, February 10, 1990, p. 217; and Nate Thayer, "PAVN troops...," *JDW*, March 3, 1990, p. 373.

decisive change in the military situation or an internal political change within one or more of the Khmer parties.

Unlike the United States, which has been content to "follow the ASEAN lead" in Southeast Asia since 1978, the PRC has pursued its own agenda. Chinese support for the Khmer Rouge is no longer unqualified, however. In 1989, notably at the Paris conference, Chinese representatives gave the Khmer Rouge only "routine support."[58] PRC backing is no longer stated in terms of ideological solidarity, but merely on the pragmatic grounds that the Khmer Rouge must participate in the settlement because they are the main military counterbalance against Vietnam and its Khmer clients.

Continued PRC backing of the Khmer Rouge and intransigence toward Vietnam are likely to be counterproductive in the long run. In the short run, it might seem advantageous to China to keep the Cambodian conflict going. Zhuang Qubing argues, however, that in the long run China has more to gain than to lose from peace in Indochina. Sino-ASEAN relations cannot depend indefinitely on Vietnam as a common enemy, because China is already seen as cynical and manipulative. Chinese participation in a peaceful settlement would help convince Southeast Asians of China's good intentions. Moreover, Zhuang argues, a neutral Cambodia is in China's best interest. Vietnamese hegemony is not acceptable, but PRC hegemony is of no use either, since it would antagonize ASEAN. Moreover, as Tian Zhongqing points out, Thailand does not want Cambodia dominated by Vietnam any more than China does. A truly neutral Cambodia would relieve Vietnam's security concerns on its western border, making Vietnam's relations with China and ASEAN less hostile. That would weaken Hanoi's dependence on the USSR, which would be welcomed by everyone concerned (including Moscow).[59]

Over the past several years, the KPR regime, led by Heng Samrin and Hun Sen, has asserted its independence in various ways. Hun Sen has gained a certain credibility as a "realistic patriot" rather than simply a "puppet" of the Vietnamese. In August 1988, Phnom Penh closed its Office of Economic and Cultural Cooperation with Vietnam and Laos, which was seen as an overt symbol of what was generally perceived as an Indochina bloc. Early in 1989, Vietnam closed its counterpart office in Hanoi. Hun Sen held meetings with Prince Sihanouk in Paris in 1988.

---

[58]Michael Field, "Starting to tango," FEER, August 10, 1989, p. 10.

[59]I am grateful to Prof. Zhuang Qubing of the China Institute of International Studies, Beijing, and to Prof. Tian Zhongqing of SIIS for these comments.

Early in 1989 he made an "unofficial visit" to Bangkok as a guest of Prime Minister Chatichai.[60]

Along with everyone else, China can take comfort in the reassertion of Khmer nationalism by the KPR. No nationalistic Cambodian government, whatever its political complexion, will be a Vietnamese (or Thai) puppet. Indeed, it is likely to be traditionally anti-Vietnamese (and anti-Thai). So there is little practical justification for China's continued backing of the Khmer Rouge. Should the Khmer Rouge regain power, or prevent a peaceful settlement, China will be blamed by ASEAN and the world.

If the Khmer Rouge regain power they will be just as murderous toward their own people as before, and probably just as aggressive toward all their neighbors. They simply will not respond to foreign control, including China's. Neither the PRC nor anybody else is going to end up with a puppet, or even a "proxy," in Cambodia. It is therefore in everybody's interest that any independent Cambodian government be neutral and non-aggressive. Some sort of coalition under Prince Sihanouk could achieve that, but only if Khmer Rouge power is constrained by all other Khmer factions, ASEAN, China, and the two superpowers.

With progress on the Cambodian issue, the focus of conflict will shift to the South China Sea. The Spratly (Nansha, Trung Sa, Kalayaan) Group is a potential battleground. On March 13, 1988, the PLA Navy sank two Vietnamese ships there.[61] Sino-Vietnamese fighting is not the only danger, either. In 1988, a Chinese warship fired at a British search-and-rescue helicopter near the disputed Paracel Islands, presumably because of mis-identification. Although China and the Philippines have agreed to shelve their conflicting claims indefinitely, Philippine and PRC warships exchanged fire and damaged each other in March 1989, owing to confusion.

Some basis for a resolution may be found in the existing bilateral agreements. China and Vietnam have separately agreed with the Philippines that any dispute over the Spratlys should be resolved peacefully. Malaysia and the Philippines are actually considering joint exploration and development of the areas where their claims overlap. The PRC's declared position on the situation is that these territorial disputes are:

---

[60]Nayan Chanda, "A Dispersion of Power," *FEER*, March 30, 1989, pp. 30-31.

[61]*Renmin Ribao* (*People's Daily*), April 1, 1988, p. 1.; *JDW*, May 28, 1988, pp. 1072-1073; and *JDW*, June 4, 1988, p. 1091.

left over by history and need time to be resolved one by one and step by step, and disputes over. . .maritime boundaries should be approached through international consultations. . . . The disputed areas with natural resources. . .in particular require negotiated settlements. . . . In this case, common exploration and sharing of resources, with the problem of sovereignty pushed aside for a certain period of time, is a fairly good approach.[62]

Deng Xiaoping himself has suggested that "countries can start first with joint development in settling territorial disputes."[63] China already has such an arrangement with Japan over the disputed Diaoyutai (Sankuku) Islands. Mark Valencia recently suggested a comprehensive, multinational cooperation council to internationalize the Spratlys and neutralize them with some sort of a multi-national council, such as the one for Antarctica.[64] Something of that sort would be in everybody's interest, including China's.

A peaceful international settlement in the Spratlys would remove an issue which otherwise is likely to increase Southeast Asian suspicion and hostility toward China. With a settlement of the Cambodian issue, there is no reason why China and Vietnam could not participate in a multinational settlement. The sticking point might be the representation of Taiwan, which occupies several islands, including Taiping Dao, the largest in the group. Taipei's policy on Chinese sovereignty in the Spratlys is exactly the same as Beijing's.

The Soviet Union remained silent about the Sino-Vietnamese clash of March 1988. Neither the USSR, nor the United States, nor any other power outside the region will take a stand on the rival claims. There is far more to lose than there is to gain by taking sides.

The South Sea island clashes and the increased capability and reach of the Chinese Navy provoke some alarm in Southeast Asia. From November 1986 to January 1987 the PLA's South Sea Fleet made a goodwill visit to Bangladesh, Sri Lanka, and Pakistan. The PLA Navy seems seriously interested in eventually acquiring an aircraft carrier, though plans were reportedly shelved for financial reasons in March 1989.[65]

---

[62]Ji Guoxing, "Current Security Issues in Southeast Asia," *Asian Survey*, Vol. 26, No. 9 (September 1986), p. 981; and "China's Indisputable Sovereignty over the Xisha and Nansha Islands," *Beijing Review*, Vol. 23, No. 7 (February 18, 1980), pp. 15-24.

[63]Wang Chunyuan and Wu Ximing, "Deng Xiaoping on Peace and War," *Beijing Review*, Vol. 32, No. 14 (April 3-9, 1989), p. 22.

[64]Mark Valencia, "All-for-Everyone Solution," *FEER*, March 30 1989, pp. 20,21.

[65]*JDW*, April 8, 1989, p. 583.

Observers throughout the region are disturbed by the recent emergence of PRC military doctrine for "limited wars." They note statements by various Chinese military thinkers approvingly citing "successful limited war operations" such as the Israeli bombing of PLO headquarters in Tunis (1985), the British Falklands (Malvinas) war (1982), and the American bombing of Libya (1986).[66] Reports appeared in 1988 of a PLA "rapid reaction force." Several battalions of commando-type troops were formed, airborne components of which will supposedly be able to deploy anywhere on China's periphery within 20 hours.[67]

Chinese sources and foreign observers alike presume that the "rapid deployment force" is intended for defense. However, "During its operations to protect border and coastal security, this contingent of special troops will accumulate experiences for operational training that will provide a reference for the modernization of regular forces."[68] The rapid deployment force is alarming to China's neighbors because it can form the basis of, and a training ground for, an offensive power projection capability.

China and the Arms Market

In the wake of the Beijing massacre, electronic upgrade of the Chinese F-8-II fighter in the United States was suspended, as were sales of counter-battery radars, artillery shell manufacturing technology, antisubmarine torpedoes, and helicopters. Contacts between the PLA and the U.S. military have been suspended, cutting off Chinese access to important training, educational, and technical help.

A likely arena for further sanctions is COCOM, the 16-member coordinating committee on export control, whose membership includes all NATO members, minus Iceland, plus Japan and Australia. COCOM has been liberalizing its restrictions on technology exports to China for the past 10 years,[69] but will likely tighten up again, or at least hold off on further liberalization. In January 1989, COCOM barred Flight Refueling,

---

[66] Gao Runqiang, "Effects of High-Tech Weapons on Local Wars," *Jiefangjun Bao* (*Liberation Army News*), January 23, 1987, p. 3. Also see Zhang Lin, with Zang Shiming, "Let Us Pursue the Study of Operations Theory in Greater Depth," *Guofang Daxue Xuebao* (*National Defense University Journal*), No. 12 (December 1, 1987), pp. 27-31; translated in JPRS-CAR-88-044 (August 5, 1988).

[67] *JDW*, June 25, 1988, p. 1274; Tai Ming Cheung, "Goodbye People's War," *FEER*, December 1, 1988, p.21; and *San Francisco Chronicle*, August 25, 1988.

[68] Chang Taiheng, "Local Conflicts and Special Troops," *Jiefangjun Bao* (*Liberation Army News*), March 14, 1986, p. 3; translated in JPRS-CAR-87-055 (November 3, 1987), p. 38.

[69] "U.S. Export Controls and China," *Gist*, Bureau of Public Affairs, Department of State, March 1989.

Ltd, of Great Britain from exporting aerial refueling technology to China. Reportedly, initial opposition came from the Japanese, who were concerned that Chinese fighter-bombers capable of aerial refueling might endanger Japan.[70] Japan was the first Northeast Asian country to express concern about increased PLA offensive capability.

Conceivably, improved relations with Moscow could lead to military technology again flowing to China from the Soviet Union. This is not likely to be very extensive, however, because the USSR's closest Asian friends are Vietnam and India, China's most likely military opponents.

The Western arms embargo on China will affect other arms flows as well. The United States has forfeited its leverage to restrain PRC arms sales.

Conclusion

It remains to be seen whether the PRC will succeed in conducting its foreign affairs as though the Democracy Movement of 1989 never happened. Relations with the West will probably not return to equilibrium for some time. In most of East Asia, however, foreign relations, for better or worse, are business as usual. Only Hong Kong and Taiwan have been much affected by the repression of the Democracy Movement. Both are more suspicious and fearful than ever, but with quite different results.

Hong Kong now seems doomed, barring an early and dramatic reversal of the political situation inside the PRC. Having been deserted by Great Britain, Hong Kong's people will desert Hong Kong if they can, taking with them the dynamism that has made it a great city. Reunification will probably be a pyrrhic victory for Beijing.

Taiwan, led by a flexible new generation, its resolve stiffened by bloody events on the mainland, shows signs of finally going its own way. Reunification now seems much less likely than it did in early 1989. Taiwan has political, economic, and human resources to maintain its de facto independence, and to weigh its alternatives into the next century.

---

[70]*Pacific Defense Reporter*, November 1986, p. 22; *JDW*, September 17, 1988, p. 603; and *JDW*, January 28, 1989, p. 137.

China's Policies Toward Vietnam and Cambodia in the 1990s[1]

by Douglas Pike

Sino-American relations, particularly those aspects having to do with the Indochinese states of Vietnam, Cambodia, and Laos, have been buffeted during the past thirty years by a wide variety of international developments, many largely unanticipated, a few totally unexpected. In reaction to these often suddenly breaking events came wide swings of policy by Washington and Beijing. In this period, which began about 1960, the United States moved from modest involvement in Southeast Asian/Indochinese affairs to deep commitment if not entrapment, to what might be called temporary disengagement, and then as it entered the 1990s, to participation in a more or less orthodox regional struggle for power. China, during this same period, moved from a regional power with limited interests to a global power with vastly greater and markedly different national security concerns. Initially, China wanted to shut the United States out of the region entirely, if possible; then, with an eye on the USSR, it came to regard the United States as a sometimes useful

[1] Source materials for this chapter were drawn chiefly from the holdings of the University of California (Berkeley) Indochina Archive. Unit VI—DRV/SRV; Section 3, *Foreign Relations*, contains some 70,000 pages of documentation on Sino-Vietnamese relations; most of this is original source material, such as official statements by Hanoi and Beijing. The full-length studies of the subject consulted include: William J. Duiker, *China and Vietnam: The Roots of Conflict*, Indochina Research Monograph No. 1 (Berkeley, CA: University of California, Institute of East Asian Studies, 1986); King C. Chen, *Vietnam and China, 1883-1954* (Princeton, NJ: Princeton University Press, 1969); Eugene K. Lawson, *The Sino-Vietnamese Conflict* (New York: Praeger, 1984); and Charles McGregor, *The Sino-Vietnamese Relationship and the Soviet Union*, Adelphi Paper No. 232 (London: International Institute for Strategic Studies, 1989). The works of Chang Pao Min, Dennis Duncanson, Donald Zagoria, and Robert A. Scalapino also contain much useful material. The author has compiled a volume entitled *Reader: Vietnam and China* (Berkeley, CA: University of California, Institute of East Asian Studies, 1990), a collection of articles and conference papers on Sino-Vietnamese relations, including his "Vietnam and China: Past, Present, and Future Relations" (1975); "New Look at Asian Foreign Policies: China and Vietnam" (1977); "Notes on the Sino-Vietnamese Border War" (April 1979); "Southeast Asia and the Superpowers: The Dust Settles" (1983); "Vietnam and Its Neighbors: Internal Influences on External Relations" (1984); "An American View of Vietnam's Relationship with China" (1985); "Vietnam and China" (1986); and "Indochina, China and the U.S.: Once and Future Triangle" (1989).

associate in the on-going great game of regional balance of power politics.[2]   Thus, over several decades the United States and China moved from an adversarial relationship, frequently in confrontation and cold war, to a harmonious association, even one that (with respect to Vietnam and Cambodia at least) could be termed a tacit alliance, the limits of which were still to be defined in the face of a yawning political and philosophical chasm between the two societies.

The spectacle was not without irony.   The Americans fought a bitter war to prevent extension of Hanoi's hegemonism throughout the Indochinese Peninsula. They were unsuccessful in this, in no small way because of Chinese contributions to their enemy's cause.   Then both the United States and China became determined to forestall further Hanoi hegemonistic activity in Cambodia and Laos, through joint and independent deterrent activities, the most extreme of which was China's "pedagogical" military incursion in 1979.

The reasons for these changing perceptions of respective national interests, with their accompanying alteration of state policies, appear to be twofold. First, there was the force of hard events of the era: external, such as the end of the Vietnam War; internal, such as the economic reform drive in China; and international, such as the changed climate in Sino-Soviet relations. Second, and as a result of these hard events, was the geopolitical reposturing by Washington and Beijing (and for that matter, by Moscow and Hanoi) to meet new national security needs. Probably there are other explanations and additional factors for this change, but whatever the reasons, the historical fact remains: over a period of three decades, events conspired to transform Chinese and American national interests with respect to Indochina from sharply hostile to more or less identical. It is not greatly overstating the case to say that since the 1979 Vietnamese invasion of Cambodia, the United States and China have had no significant quarrels with respect to Hanoi or to the struggle in Cambodia.   Rather, their respective policies have shown a mutuality of national interest rare in modern international relations.

As we enter the 1990s, the question is whether this harmony, this identity of interests, will continue.   Will the policymakers in Washington and Beijing still see eye to eye with respect to Hanoi's behavior in general and its foreign policies in particular?   The great variable here, which makes prognosis difficult, is the future character of the top Beijing leadership.   Whatever the changed nature of this leadership becomes,

---

[2]For an appreciation of how stark has been this reversal in Chinese strategic thinking, see R.B. Smith's "China and Southeast Asia: The Revolutionary Perspective, 1951," *Journal of Southeast Asian Studies*, Vol. XIX, No. 1 (March 1988).

however, it is unlikely that there will ever be a return to the cold war condition of the 1950s.

Historical Overview

The association of Vietnamese to Chinese has roots deep in history. It has always been complex, unlike, say, the starkly elemental relationship of Vietnamese and Russians. In examining this deep association of a thousand years standing, it is useful to separate the factors involved into two general categories: those in what may be called the subliminal dimension, having to do with the affective level of the relationship; and the more finite level of material interests.[3] The first is far more important than the second, although they are intricately bound together.

Both the Vietnamese and the Chinese have profound senses of history, which means the relationship inevitably is heavily burdened by historical influences. Vietnamese historians viewing China see it as possessed of a self-image born of a sense of being unique, one they treat with a variety of terms: great hegemonism, Han chauvinism, ethno-linguistic imperialism, and, most commonly, "Chineseness."[4] China's self-image long ago created in the Chinese an implacable view of the world. China was different and therefore superior, granting it the right to act as Heaven's monitor and supervisor of the destinies of the peoples living along the perimeter of the Middle Kingdom. This, in turn, imposed on the rimland barbarians, such as the Vietnamese, an obligation of deference to this Confucian order of things.[5]

The Vietnamese, themselves steeped in Confucian thought, tended to share this perception. For centuries they recognized the mentor relationship and extended gestures of deference, at least symbolic ones.

---

[3]The subliminal level of Sino-Vietnamese relations is explored in some detail in Douglas Pike, "Vietnam and Its Neighbors: Internal Influences on External Relations," in Karl D. Jackson, Sukhumbhand Paribatra, and J. Soedjati Djiwandono, editors, *ASEAN in Regional and Global Context*, Research Papers and Policy Studies No. 18 (Berkeley, CA: University of California, Institute of East Asian Studies, 1986).

[4]A phenomenon not confined to the Vietnamese. Go anywhere in the world—Denmark, Brazil, South Africa, Israel—and speak of "Chineseness" and your audience instantly accepts the transcendental sense of things Chinese, the notion of China not as another culture or nation but as some self-contained planet.

[5]This may strike Westerners, viewing it through the egalitarian prism, as haughty arrogance:

> There is the House of Haves and the House of Have Nots.
> God named the Haves as caretakers of the Have Nots.
> This shepherding is a divine decree laid on the betters.
> "And surely you know when you are among your betters?"

Carl Sandberg, *The People Yes* (New York: Harcourt, Brace, 1936), p.53.

74

As late as the 1880s the Court in Annam each lunar New Year would send to the Emperor in Peking a small lacquered box containing a single gold coin. While the Vietnamese always fiercely fended off what they considered excessive Chinese intrusiveness, they absorbed the culture and its underlying sense of substantive deference rooted in the understanding that rulers of Sinitic-type countries adjacent to China must not make certain major decisions without first consulting with Peking.

Fear of China has pervaded Vietnamese thinking, as the direct result of historical experience. The Chinese occupied Vietnam at the time of Christ and spent 900 years in *han-hwa* (sinoization) efforts, but the Nam Viets alone among the Hundred Yueh (tribes) of southern China successfully resisted assimilation. The Chinese returned again in the 13th and 15th centuries in campaigns of conquest. Various hegemonistic efforts persisted through the next several centuries. As late as 1953 China's name for its main road leading into Vietnam was *Chennankuan* (Suppressing the South Pass). In 1979 China sent 180,000 "pedagogic" invaders into Vietnam.

However, and to a large extent this has always been the case, the Vietnamese fear of China has not been based primarily on physical threat. Rather, it has taken a more subtle form of fear of emasculation—a feared loss of Vietnamese identity, of Vietnam's culture smothered by the awesome force of Chinese civilization. It is a genuine fear, even given a benign China.

Coupled with this fear, and representing an additional complicating factor in the relationship, is the fact that the Vietnamese have always admired, respected, and emulated the Chinese. More than most Vietnamese care to admit, even to themselves, there is the suspicion that what is best about Vietnam is of Chinese origin. Vietnam in fact greatly imitated China's art, architecture, music, and literature. The Vietnamese legal and educational systems and governmental and social institutions copied those of China—not just old imperial China, but China today. For a cultured but nationalistic Vietnamese taking pride in Vietnam's heritage, this buried suspicion, that Vietnam is but a "smaller dragon" and little more than a pale carbon copy of China, is a hard thought to accept with equanimity.

Because of these countervailing influences, it cannot be said that the Vietnamese attitude toward China is merely the negative product of fear, suspicion, and occasional hatred. Nor can it be said that the Vietnamese, either collectively or individually, hate the Chinese. Rather, the Vietnamese attitude more closely resembles the modern day psychiatric concept of a love-hate relationship that both seeks and rejects. It is this dual quality that lends such complexity to the association. In any event, it is a highly durable one which can be counted on as a firm behavioral pattern that will manifest itself in future Hanoi foreign policymaking with respect to China.

Vietnam's posture toward China has always been made worse by the Vietnamese national character trait of suspicion and distrust, a product of its long heritage. Always the Vietnamese anticipate betrayal and, as their thousand-year history demonstrates, usually they are not disappointed. The result is, individually and collectively, an ingrained inability to trust. Hence, fear of China as an ever-plotting villain, and a tendency to interpret each Chinese act in terms of worst possible motive, make up the normal Vietnamese response.

What is required in the 1990s is to define a new relationship between Vietnam and China. The Vietnamese say it must be one based on equity, as egalitarianism is connoted in Asia, which puts an end to the now outdated *sensei*-pupil relationship. The Vietnamese argue they deserve this because of their new status, earned by victory in war. The Chinese do not consider that the associational context has changed all that much. The Vietnamese expect the Chinese to modify their attitudes, including the notion of the rimland barbarian's deference to the Center of Heaven. The Chinese expect the Vietnamese to respect historical attitudinal obligations, particularly the principle of harmonious deference.

A sorting out process has gone on between the two since the end of the Vietnam War, and will continue however long it takes to define a new relationship. It should be understood that this process is no mere exercise in cultural exchange, but is a very real political and strategic struggle with high stakes and profound meaning for the future.

Finite Issues

Considerable attention has been devoted above to the affective or subliminal level of the Sino-Vietnamese relationship. This was done for several reasons. First, while in most bilateral diplomatic relationships which exist around the world, material factors far outweigh the cultural, in the Sino-Vietnamese relationship the opposite is the case. The affective dimension, certainly for the Vietnamese, counts for far more than any finite issue, and will continue to do so in the future. The Confucian process of defining relations—which in this case turns on whether the ancient *sensei*-pupil association is to be changed or preserved—strikes most Westerners as an obscure exercise in Oriental metaphysics. Actually it is the ultimate reality. Second, this dimension of the relationship is generally overlooked or ignored by outsiders doing geopolitical studies, either because they see no relevance or because they are uncomfortable working at this level of security analysis. In either case, they do so to their own ultimate regret. Third, the subliminal level relationship is highly enduring, which means that while finite issues may come and go, the culturally derived factors will linger on, into the 1990s and beyond.

The multitude of finite or material issues that beset the Sino-Vietnamese relationship after the end of the Vietnam War can be expressed best in terms of the grievances held by the two parties. China has had three major grievances. First, there was Hanoi's intimate embrace of the USSR, incautiously throwing itself into dependency on Moscow gold, and thus opening itself up to opportunistic Soviet exploitation that eventually led to what amounted to a Soviet-Vietnamese alliance against China.[6] Second, there was Hanoi's extended intrusions into the affairs of Cambodia and Laos, culminating in the ultimate act of denial of sovereignty, invasion of Cambodia, and installation of a puppet government. These intrusions, the Chinese suspected, were only Hanoi's first move in the political reconfiguration of the Indochina Peninsula. At the end of the road lay a Hanoi-dominated Federation of Indochina, which would deny China's legitimate national security interests in the region. Worse, it was an act of pure humiliation, designed to remove the Chinese presence entirely from Phnom Penh and, if possible, from Vientiane. Third, there were brutal Hanoi programs and policies of ugly racist overtone inside Vietnam. Sino-Vietnamese, some of them third-generation, were harassed into leaving as "boat people" or trucked to the Chinese border and pushed across.[7]

Vietnam's grievances against China are more generalized. In simple terms it is Chinese aggression, broadly defined. The 1979 Sino-Vietnamese border war was merely a more visible form of this aggression. Since about 1977 China has determinedly conducted a cold war against Vietnam—not simply a border war and a war among the off-shore islands, but massive off-the-battlefield efforts to frustrate Hanoi's domestic policies and vilify Vietnam's image abroad, through campaigns in various international forums, such as the United Nations and ASEAN (Association of South East Asian Nations) meetings, and in Hanoi's bilateral relations with the USSR. Through these efforts, China seeks to isolate Vietnam in the international economic arena and impede its economic development. Thus it is a "war" that is not only military, but also diplomatic, economic, political, and psychological.

---

[6]Soviet-Vietnamese relations are treated in the author's full-length study, *Vietnam and the USSR: Anatomy of an Alliance* (Boulder, CO: Westview, 1987).

[7]These number an estimated 250,000, most of whom are still living in specially constructed villages in Yunnan province.

The Hanoi press, seeking a generic term to describe all of this anti-Vietnamese diatribe, chose the term "multifaceted war of sabotage." Over the years it has published voluminous accounts of the strategy, as have the Chinese, although on a lesser scale. However, little about it is known abroad chiefly because of a lack of attention. This multifaceted war of sabotage, when analyzed as a strategy, seems uniquely Sino-Vietnamese. It makes extensive use of the famed Vietnamese concept *dau tranh* (struggle), which is derived from Chinese thought—a vast and amorphous notion of state policy implemented through a combination of protracted armed struggle and political struggle which erases the line between war and politics. This "struggle" involves a semi-secret border and naval war, a disinformation campaign in the name of motivating and mobilizing outsider support, systematic development of diplomatic support, and international economic sabotage.

The "multifaceted war of sabotage" is more than a cold war or a war of nerves, but less than a limited war. At the Sino-Vietnamese frontier the "war" consists of sporadic campaigns of harassment by each side, chiefly employing artillery and mortars and trans-border patrol probes. Border action involves various clandestine Chinese activities—hence the term "sabotage"—conducted for the most part by ethnic minorities traditionally hostile to Vietnam or with familial ties in China.

The best way to appreciate the magnitude of this effort by China—this central grievance of Vietnam against China—is to read the following account offered by a major Hanoi military figure:

> The Chinese expansionists and hegemonists pursue a multifaceted war of sabotage which they hope to "win without fighting," that is exhausting Vietnam's resources, crippling its economy, creating political chaos and internal disorder so, without firing a shot, we are forced to become their vassals . . . . In this multifaceted war of sabotage, the enemy attacks us in many fields: economically, politically, ideologically and culturally. They do everything possible to undermine our national defense system and our military potential. They use dangerous malicious tricks to foment rebellion and a *coup d'etat* when the time is ripe. They routinely send armed forces across our northern border along with espionage agents, commandos, aircraft, and so forth. They seek to exert pressure, harass, provoke. They look for methods to distort our military draft, cause a longing for peace, encourage our troops to desert, and youth to evade the draft . . . . The most deadly form of this multifaceted war of sabotage is economic. They use lackeys to sabotage machinery, set warehouses afire, sabotage production discipline and the managerial mechanism, so as to stagnate production. They encourage smuggling, speculation and hoarding, and cause a gold "hemorrhage" to undermine our monetary system . . . . China undermines our economic policies, sows skepticism to cause our people to lose faith in the Party's economic leadership. It distorts our relationship with other

countries and our practice of international economic cooperation. China frantically fixes embargoes, pressures private capitalist individuals and companies not to sign contracts with us, or to cancel, postpone or reduce them. The Chinese sabotage our warehouses, seaports, industrial installations. They organize gangs of smugglers to bring in contraband and take out gold and gems. They also introduce chemical poisons, insects, and micro-organisms to injure food production. . . . They conduct intense psychological war to distort Party and State policies. They secretly send reactionary cultural products into our country to sow the seeds of a decadent lifestyle, especially among youth. They provoke dissatisfaction and political opposition. They bribe or exert pressure on corrupt elements in the State apparatus to get them to serve as their lackeys. All these schemes are designed to erode the confidence of the people, confuse our friends, paralyze our revolutionary will, undermine the solidarity of PAVN and the Party, the special solidarity among Vietnam, Laos and Kampuchea, and the solidarity and cooperation between Vietnam and the USSR. . . .[8]

Whatever else, the Chinese strategy in the "war of multifaceted sabotage" clearly is coherent and well thought out. However, its effects are difficult to estimate. Vietnam's response, in effect its counter-strategy, is built around mobilizing its border population, carrying out extensive nationwide motivational campaigns, and constantly asserting the administrative centrality of party leadership. To this end, it has an estimated 600,000 military and paramilitary forces stationed in the border area. Military journals stress the importance of centralized strategic planning rather than leaving the response to local PAVN commanders and provincial officials. They call for intensified internal security controls, particularly among ethnic minority peoples along the border.

Hanoi theoretical military journals contend that Beijing's rationale for employing this strategy is China's determination to extend its hegemony throughout the region, if not throughout the entire world. China's step-by-step plan for this, the Hanoi military analysis continues, is fourfold: to become a nuclear power; to build a "special forces belt" of insurgent, proxy, largely ethnic minority support elements in the arc of its border from Afghanistan to Vietnam; to upgrade the PLA, the most important of China's "four modernizations"; and to insure that China's defenses can cope with any foreign invasion. This "world conquest" scheme, the

---

[8]Drawn from Nhuan Vu, "Concerning Chinese Military Strategy" and Thien Nhan, "Fighting the Enemy's War of Economic Sabotage," in *Tap Chi Cong San*, August 1982. For additional discussion of the PAVN High Command's view of Chinese strategic intent, see Major General Dang Kinh, "Building District Military Fortresses Along the Northern Border," and Central Committee agit-prop expert Nam Huy's article, "Fighting the War of Sabotage on the Ideological Front in the Northern Border Provinces," both in *Tap Chi Quan Doi Nhan Dan*, January 1983; PAVN Maj. General Pham Minh Tam's "Defense of the North Border, " in *Tap Chi Quan Doi Nhan Dan*, July 1987; and Quyet Thang's "China's Defense Strategy to the Year 2000," in *Tap Chi Quoc Phong Toan Dan*, June 1988.

analysis concludes, is being blocked by the USSR and Vietnam. For this reason, the matter is of major importance to other countries in the region, and they should fully support the Soviet-Vietnamese defensive effort.[9]

From our examination three conclusions seem clear: this multifaceted war of sabotage is more than a festering border war; it is costly for Vietnam in terms of resources; and in one form or another—actual operations or an ever present potential—it will continue into the 1990s.

Hanoi's second chief grievance concerns Cambodia and, to a lesser degree, Laos, and involves Chinese efforts to frustrate what Hanoi officials consider necessary Khmer and Lao relationships to serve Vietnamese national security, which in no way threaten China. What the Vietnamese want from their two neighbors, at the minimum, appears to be three-fold. First, they want primacy in bilateral relations so that neither Phnom Penh nor Vientiane ever makes a major decision, particularly external, without first clearing it with Hanoi. Second, Hanoi wants assurances that neither country will develop close relations with other countries, particularly any sort of military alliance. Third, the Vietnamese want in each of the two capitals an element—probably a faction in the local Communist Party—consisting of indigenous Lao and Khmer officials who would have an allegiance to Hanoi. These individuals would not be subversives, simply "Hanoi's boys" in Phnom Penh and Vientiane. Such an element currently exists with the Pathet Lao as a result of early recruitment and long association. In Cambodia the mechanism is being created in the newly reorganized Khmer Communist Party.

It seems probable that Hanoi's ultimate goal is a Federation of Indochina. Ho Chi Minh talked openly of the idea in the 1950s. Arguments can be made for and against it in terms of the respective Khmer and Lao interests. A federation would bring together some 70 million people traditionally suspicious of China if not hostile to it. Obviously, the Chinese would prefer to deal with three Indochinese states rather than a single one. The real question is to what lengths Beijing is willing to go to prevent a federation. It is not an issue that must be faced immediately, but the idea of federation will be a central factor in future Sino-Vietnamese relations.

There are those in Washington and elsewhere who expect a future Vietnamese-Chinese confrontation, even war, over the offshore islands

---

[9]For analysis of the tactics and strategy employed by both sides in this "multifaceted war of sabotage," see Douglas Pike's "Vietnam's Relationship with China," in Robert A. Scalapino and Chen Qimao, editors, *Pacific-Asian Issues: American and Chinese Views*, Research and Policy Studies No. 17 (Berkeley, CA: University of California, Institute of East Asian Studies, 1986).

in the South China Sea; they believe the confrontation will not be deliberate, but will result from blunder or miscalculation. Certainly such a conflict would not be in the rational self-interest of either side; if common sense prevails, there will be no war. But the analysts are quite right in pointing to the strong emotional, non-rational elements present in both camps. Extraordinary intransigence exists between China and Vietnam over the various small dots which Chinese sailors traditionally call the Isles of Dangerous Places. China considers its claims to the Spratly and Paracel archipelagos to be clear and just. Vietnam portrays the problem as deliberate Chinese provocation. Virtually everything about these islands is in dispute: their history, past and present ownership, even their names. What is not contested is the potential oil reserve value of the sedimentary basin beneath them.

For more than a decade, a struggle of rhetoric and symbolic gesture, of the sort so important in Asia, has gone on unabated, keeping the offshore island issue in the forefront of consciousness in both countries. Hanoi issued postage stamps bearing maps claiming the islands. Similar maps on billboards were erected near the Chinese embassy in Hanoi. In their major speeches, SRV military officials regularly include references to the need to defend Vietnam's territorial integrity. The Chinese approach has been to stake out a 2000-year claim to the islands. Beijing scholarly journals report new archaeological findings on the islands that prove Chinese administrative control dating back to the Han Dynasty. Similar claims, some based on 17th century geography textbooks, have been made by the Vietnamese. There have also been naval clashes in which the Vietnamese took casualties.[10]

Most China watchers are of the opinion that Beijing will brook no challenge to its claims to these islands and, if necessary, China will fight for them. It seems equally clear that Vietnam, while seeking to avoid a show-down, will never voluntarily relinquish control of the islands now held, nor its claim to them. Beijing's and Hanoi's statements on the islands are never couched in the language of compromise. Neither side, judging by their public statements and behavior, seems willing to seek an amicable settlement.

Territorial disputes and other finite issues standing between Vietnam and China do not differ much in character from other bilateral disputes within the region. They are a form of Sino-Vietnamese competition for spheres of influence in Southeast Asia and, as such, appear to be inevitable. In

---

[10]Hanoi's current strategic position on the offshore islands was set forth by the SRV Navy Commander-in-Chief, Admiral Giap Van Cuong, "The People's Navy in Defense of Vietnam's Sovereignty in the South China Sea," *Tap Chi Quoc Phong Toan* (Hanoi), February 1989.

the future, China will seek to contain what it suspects are Hanoi's imperial dreams, being particularly alert to evidence of new Vietnamese-Soviet collusion. Vietnam will continue to press its claims for status, mostly symbolic ones, as the search for its historical destiny continues. However, this will not go on in isolation. Rather, the bilateral Sino-Vietnamese struggle for power will be conducted within the Southeast Asia regional balance of power arena, which in turn falls within the broader context of superpower politics.[11]

Hanoi Leadership

Anyone predicting the course and nature of Sino-Vietnamese relations in the 1990s, as with all prognostication involving either of these two countries, does so at his own peril. The history of Vietnam in this century—indeed the history of Asia—is filled with events which no one anticipated or predicted. The primary reason for this appears to be the large number of imponderables always at work.

One of these imponderables, the most important as far as Vietnam is concerned, is the leadership in Hanoi. Since the death of Vietnamese Communist Party General Secretary Le Duan in July 1986, the highest level—that is, the Politburo—leadership in Hanoi has been involved in an intense, complex political struggle, one which, as of this writing, has not yet run its course. The resulting turbulence in both party and state leadership in the late 1980s was intensified by the steady departure of the "old guard" figures. Four of the Politburo's "inner circle of five" have died or retired in 1988 and 1989. This added a new dimension to the political infighting—over which party officials were to be elevated to the Politburo/Central Committee as well as what type of individuals (from what backgrounds) were to be recruited.

As the 1980s ended, it appeared that the Politburo/Central Committee in Hanoi was dividing into four major factions: (1) the reformers, known earlier as the pragmatist faction, who held that Vietnamese society must be renovated, opened up, "democratized," to enable the system to survive into the next century; (2) the neo-conservatives, known earlier as the ideologue faction, whose chief concern was the risks involved in reform—while agreeing that change was required, they feared that

---

[11]The regional impact of the Vietnam-China relationship is discussed by Sarasin Viraphol in his chapter, "The People's Republic of China and Southeast Asia: A Security Consideration for the 1980s," in Robert A. Scalapino and Jusuf Wanandi, editors, *Economic, Political and Security Issues in the 1980s*, Research Papers and Policy Studies No. 7 (Berkeley, CA: University of California, Institute of East Asian Studies, 1982). See also Lucian Pye's "China and Southeast Asia" in the same volume.

reform would introduce unintended change that could have catastrophic effects on Vietnamese internal socio-political institutions and on foreign policy; (3) the military, specifically the three generals in the Politburo whose interests are geopolitics, foreign military assistance, and those foreign policies that impinge on national security, such as relations with the USSR, PAVN withdrawal from Cambodia, and China policy; and (4) the technocrats, also commonly labeled in the press as the "bureaucrats" (i.e., with State rather than Party interests) or "economists" (i.e., with direct or indirect responsibilities in the economic sector). Doctrinal infighting therefore was not simply between reformer and conservative, but was a four-way struggle in which the military and technocrat "swing" forces would vote with the reformers or conservatives, depending on the specific issue.

The most disputed doctrinal issue in this factional infighting was the wisdom of change versus the need for continuity, and within this debate, the acceptable degree of risk to be taken in introducing change. This had particular application to future China policy: How far are the Chinese to be trusted? Most of the other central policy issues facing the Hanoi leadership also had some meaning with respect to China as well as the United States, particularly those in the economic sector: What should be the proper allocation of economic resources; how should outside economic aid and trade be developed; and how can Vietnam best insure access to military arms and hardware, since there are no arms factories in Vietnam?

It is this collection of imponderables, each of which will impinge on Hanoi policymaking, that makes it so hazardous to try to predict the nature and course of Sino-Vietnamese relations in the 1990s.

The Future Triangle

What is the meaning of all this for the United States and the future of Sino-American relations? As we have noted, the history of U.S.-Chinese relations, with respect to Vietnam, Cambodia, and Laos, following the end of the Vietnam War, was a remarkably harmonious one, with virtually no serious policy differences. This was not deliberate; rather, it was the logical result of unfolding events, most importantly Vietnam's 1979 invasion of Cambodia. The relationship became an isosceles triangle—the two equal sides being China and the United States, and the short side, Vietnam. The question as we enter the 1990s is whether this common Sino-American outlook on Indochina will continue, or whether there are likely to be divergences of interest—that is, will the triangle remain isosceles or become equilateral?

In all likelihood, Washington and Beijing will continue to pursue similar policies with regard to Indochina affairs.[12] Both will be obliged to deal with the singular Vietnamese diplomatic behavior and foreign policies, even if Hanoi leaders and policies change. Both will remain devoted to preserving the sovereignty of Kampuchea and Laos against whatever efforts Hanoi makes to "federate" the peninsula. Both will continue to press for a "distancing" of Hanoi from Moscow and ending Vietnam's excessive dependence on the USSR.

In addition, both China and the United States will continue to have certain bilateral policy problems with Hanoi which do not particularly involve other parties: for China, the border and offshore island territorial disputes; for the United States, the resolution of the missing military personnel issue left over from the Vietnam war. Such issues may eventually be resolved in the 1990s, but since they are distinctly bilateral in nature, they will not be of particular concern to outsiders, assuming none devolves into a "flash point" crisis.

Sino-American differences may develop over diplomatic approach—how best to influence Hanoi, whether with carrot, with stick, or with a combination of the two. There could be differences over the degree of their respective involvements in Indochinese affairs, over the emphasis that should be placed on regional organizations, including ASEAN, over the role of Indochinese integration, and over the relationship of the USSR to the China-Vietnam-U.S. triangle.

These matters essentially are unfathomable at this writing since they turn on global trends and developments, such as co-existence, arms control, nonalignment, and economic interdependence—indeed, the "death of communism" itself—all underscoring the fact that the future foreign policies of both the United States and China with respect to Vietnam in the 1990s are indeterminate. They will also depend on the kind of leadership that eventually emerges in Hanoi; on developments along the Beijing-Moscow axis; on the kind of settlement that is finally achieved in Cambodia; and on internal Vietnamese affairs, above all on whether Vietnam is able finally to solve its short-run economic problems and begin true economic development. Chinese and American policies will be shaped by all of these developments, but beyond this we cannot predict what the future holds.

---

[12]For an authoritative statement of current Chinese official thinking on the 1990s, see Tian Zhongqing, "The Prospects of Kampuchea Issue and the Changes of Vietnam's Relations with Big Powers and ASEAN in the Post-Kampuchea Era," and Jin Xudong, "An Opportunity for a Political Settlement of the Kampuchea Issue is in the Offing," papers presented at the Third Conference of the Institute of East Asian Studies (University of California, Berkeley) and the Shanghai Institute of Strategic Studies Conference, Maanshan, China, May 15-18, 1989.

The Sino-American Relationship:
A Chinese Perspective

by Ding Xinghao

Good relations between China and the United States are of vital importance to peace and stability in East Asia and the Pacific, and at the global level as well, and would serve the national interests of both countries. Relations between the two countries in the 1950s and 1960s, however, were characterized by hostility to, and isolation from, each other. China and the United States began to move toward a rapprochement in late 1969, and, despite continuing differences over Taiwan and other issues, the two nations managed to maintain a steady and improving relationship for the next twenty years until the spring of 1989. If there had not been the June 1989 events in Beijing, the Sino-American relationship, as expected by a majority of the two peoples and their leaders, might have entered a new decade of consultation and cooperation. However, the intense strains resulting from the Tiananmen Square events have brought U.S.-Chinese relations to their lowest point since 1972. One cannot help wondering what the real factors are behind the fluctuations in our relations. The purpose of this paper is to assess these factors so that we may better understand the past, the present, and the future of this relationship.

The Motives Behind the Initial Opening

The process of normalization of relations between the United States and China that began in the late 1960s was a product of major foreign policy readjustments by the two parties. In 1969, soon after he took office as U.S. President, Richard Nixon together with his national security adviser, Dr. Henry Kissinger, began to translate into action their belief that tremendous changes had taken place in the world situation since the end of the Second World War, and that the United States must respond with new policies. The most striking of these changes was the appearance of five world centers of power that were transforming the bipolar world. They decided to maintain the leading position of the United States in the world by taking advantage of differences among the powers, and by maneuvering among them to achieve a global balance of power. What struck Nixon most was the emergence of the Soviet Union as a very powerful and threatening rival. As a result, he decided to try to increase U.S. leverage in dealing with Moscow by improving relations with China. After his inauguration, President Nixon indicated that as the United States was not prepared to mount an effort sufficient to win the Vietnam war, the United States must end the conflict as soon as possible, before it was too late to save face. Dr. Kissinger put it bluntly that "an opening to China might help us end the agony of that war."[1]

On China's part, an increased sense of threat from the Soviet Union made Chairman Mao Zedong and Premier Zhou Enlai willing to end the long confrontation with the United States so as to counter Soviet expansionism. Meanwhile, driven by its sacred cause of "the reunification of the motherland," China's leadership hoped that a reconciliation between China and the United States would help over time to resolve the Taiwan problem. Furthermore, by the end of the 1960s China had embarked upon a repudiation of the "leftist" trend of thought, trying to reduce this extremist influence over its diplomacy, and by so doing to resume and expand contacts with foreign countries. Finally, by improving Sino-American relations, China sought to remove the obstacles thrown up by the United States to keep China from actively participating in world affairs.

There were many common motivations behind the American and Chinese decisions to open the door to each other at the initial stage, a fact that must not be underestimated. But one also must not overlook the different interests and objectives of the two countries separated by a "deep historical, cultural and political chasm,"[2] which tended from the very beginning to give rise to misunderstanding, miscalculation, and frustration.

Strategic Interests

The United States and China achieved a breakthrough in their relationship for a number of reasons, but the strategic one was the most important for both parties at the very beginning. Former U.S. President Nixon recalled in a *New York Times* article: "The key factor that brought us [U.S. and PRC] together . . . was our common concern with the Soviet threat and our recognition that we had a better chance of containing that

---

[1]Henry Kissinger, *White House Years* (Boston, MA: Little, Brown, 1979), p. 194.

[2]George R. Packard, "The Policy Paper—China Policy for the Next Decade," in U. Alexis Johnson, et al., editors, *China Policy for the Next Decade: The Atlantic Council's Committee on China Policy* (Weston, MA: Oelgeschlager, Gunn & Hain, 1984), p.1.

threat if we replaced hostility with cooperation between Peking and Washington."[3]

The "chance" turned up when the military conflict on Zhenbao Island broke out in March 1969. This incident was a turning point in Sino-Soviet relations, for it indicated that the nature of the differences between the two nations had escalated from ideological debate to military conflicts. Zhenbao provided clear evidence to the Americans that the Sino-Soviet relationship had deteriorated to such an extent that it was not reconcilable, and to the Chinese that they were faced with an immediate threat from the north, and that their principal adversary was not the United States but the Soviet Union.

Soon after the Zhenbao Island incident a number of signals were exchanged between the United States and China. The Nixon Administration, in July 1969, lifted restrictions on travel and bilateral trade between the two countries. An agreement was reached to resume diplomatic talks at the ambassadorial level in Warsaw on January 20, 1970. During his conversation with an old American friend, Edgar Snow, on December 18, 1970, Chairman Mao expressed his willingness to meet with President Nixon. Then the American ping-pong team was invited to visit China in April 1971. All these events led to Dr. Kissinger's secret visit to Beijing on July 9, 1971, and President Nixon's subsequent trip to China, during which the first Sino-U.S. joint communique was signed in Shanghai on February 28, 1972.

The Sino-Soviet split and the Sino-American rapprochement were widely regarded as benefiting the U.S. global position. As a result, the impact of the Vietnam debacle upon the United States was reduced, SALT I and some other agreements with Soviet President Leonid Brezhnev were signed, and a period of detente with the Soviet Union followed.

Sino-American relations, however, have stagnated since the early 1970s. Normalization of relations, including establishment of formal diplomatic ties between the two countries, took six more years—from the year when President Nixon made his first trip to Beijing to 1978—partly because of the internal political climate relating to the Watergate crisis in the United States and the continuing "cultural revolution" turmoil in China. Most Chinese believe that the delay was attributable primarily to the policies of Nixon and Kissinger, the consummate strategists, who felt that the more relaxed tensions between the United States and the Soviet Union became, the less important strategically China became. Logically, they

[3]Richard Nixon, "America and China: The Next Ten Years," *New York Times*, October 11, 1982, p.419.

were not inclined to take substantial steps toward normalization of relations by making unnecessary concessions over the Taiwan problem.

During Jimmy Carter's years in the White House, beginning in 1977, Soviet expansionism became an increasing problem—first in Angola, South Yemen, and the Horn of Africa, and then in Afghanistan at the end of 1979. The Carter Administration was convinced that a genuinely cooperative relationship between China and the United States would "greatly enhance the stability of the Far East and that, more generally, it would be to U.S. advantage in the global competition with the Soviet Union." Therefore, from the American strategic standpoint, "normalization [of the Sino-U.S. relationship] was desirable."[4]

While visiting the United States in early 1979, immediately after the normalization, Vice Premier Deng Xiaoping stressed that "the interests of the people of both countries and that of world peace require us to view Sino-American relations from the overall world situation and with a long-term and strategic viewpoint."[5] He even talked about a broad "united front"[6] formed to oppose Soviet hegemonism represented by interference in Afghanistan's internal affairs, support for the Vietnamese occupation of Cambodia, and other expansionist policies. Clearly, the Soviet factor and other strategic considerations played a most important role in shaping the development of Sino-American relations during the ten years from the breakthrough in bilateral ties to the establishment of formal diplomatic relations.

However, when the Reagan Administration took office in 1981, its China policy seemed self-contradictory. On the one hand, "determined to counter the growing Soviet threat, the Reagan Administration, during the first two years of its term, pursued a strategic alliance with the PRC even more vigorously than Carter."[7] On the other hand, the attitude it took toward mainland China and Taiwan was in sharp contrast with that of its immediate predecessor. President Reagan declared a "full implementation" of the Taiwan Relations Act, threatened to sell more sophisticated arms to Taiwan, and warned that China should not interfere with U.S. policy toward Taiwan. To many Chinese, it was American "wishful thinking" that in exchange for strategic cooperation from the

---

[4]Zbigniew Brzezinski, *Power and Principle: Memoirs of the National Security Advisor, 1977-1981* (New York: Farrar, Straus & Giroux, 1983), pp. 196-197.

[5]Toast by Vice Premier Deng Xiaoping at a state banquet given by President Carter, *People's Daily*, January 29, 1979.

[6]Vice Premier Deng Xiaoping interviewed by an American journalist, *Newsweek*, February 5, 1979.

[7]Martin L. Lasater, *U.S. Policy Toward China's Reunification* (Washington, D.C.: Heritage Foundation, 1988).

United States, China would have to "swallow the bitter pill of Taiwan." Some American friends of China thought that Reagan's attitude "made China worry about the possibility of bilateral ties returning to the Dulles era."[8] The real situation was not that serious, but the tension resulting from it forced China to reconsider U.S. reliability. For this reason, as well as Beijing's reassessment of the military balance between the United States and the Soviet Union, China began to move toward an independent foreign policy. In Chinese eyes, the world situation had changed. In the early seventies the Soviet Union had strengthened its armed forces and had become a threat to many countries. Because of the impressive U.S. military buildup during the first Reagan Administration, the military competition between the two superpowers had reached a new equilibrium.

According to the "independent and peaceful foreign policy" articulated by General Secretary Hu Yaobang in late 1982, China in its foreign relations would not be dependent on any superpower or power groups, nor would it be closely aligned with any countries, whether large or small. While continuing to broaden Sino-American ties, China moved gradually to improve relations with the Soviet Union. In the second half of 1982, China and the Soviet Union began consultations at the vice ministerial level.

The United States, for its part, also began to adjust its foreign policies, its Asian policy in particular. The Reagan Administration realized that China could not cooperate with America on all strategic issues, especially those concerning the third world, and concluded that it should not overestimate China's role in America's global strategy. While downgrading China's strategic importance, the Reagan Administration placed more emphasis on the role of Japan as a cornerstone of U.S. Asian policy.[9]

These mutual adjustments resulted from both parties recognizing that the strategic or Soviet factor was not the sole basis for Sino-American relations. In February 1983, U.S. Secretary of State George Shultz visited Beijing to explore new ways to improve bilateral relations. Since then, the United States has stopped using the term "strategic relations" to describe U.S.-China ties, and both the United States and China have tended to stress the importance of the growth of economic, political, and cultural relations between them. Following the exchange of visits of Premier Zhao Ziyang and President Reagan in early 1984, which was

---

[8]Henry Kissinger, "The Key Point of Shultz's Visit: Can U.S. and China Coordinate Their Views on the World?," *International Herald Tribune*, February 2, 1983, p.6.

[9]George Shultz, speech delivered at the World Affairs Council, San Francisco, March 5, 1983.

regarded as a turning point, Sino-American relations began to develop on a steady course.

Starting from the mid-1980s, remarkable changes in the world situation have been under way, and the balance of power between the United States and the Soviet Union has shifted in favor of the United States. Soviet General Secretary Gorbachev, on assuming power in March 1985 and with political reform and economic growth as top priorities on his agenda, undertook a series of diplomatic initiatives. Four summits between Reagan and Gorbachev were held from 1985 to 1988, and during this period the INF Treaty was negotiated, signed, and ratified. Following the new detente between the two superpowers, Sino-Soviet relations also improved substantially when Beijing and Moscow made some progress in negotiations over the three major obstacles: the Soviet military presence in Afghanistan, Soviet aid to the Vietnamese Army in Kampuchea, and the high levels of Soviet troops along the Sino-Soviet border. Subsequently, the need for the United States and China to deal jointly with the Soviet threat has decreased, and the importance of strategic-triangle relations has declined as well—all as a result of the diminishing Soviet threat to the outside world.

Nonetheless, China and the United States share a common interest in maintaining peace and stability in the Asian-Pacific region. For a number of years, China and the United States have adopted largely parallel policies toward Afghanistan, Northeast Asia, Southeast Asia, and South Asia, and have contributed significantly to the stability of these regions. Although China is not a global power, it is a regional power with some global influence. For various reasons, it may be expected that the United States will continue for many years to share common strategic and security interests with China.

First, if the world is indeed evolving from a bipolar to a multipolar system, the process can be said to have started in Asia. Of the five world centers of power, four are in the Asian-Pacific region. Northeast Asia is the very place where the interests of the four major powers — the United States, the Soviet Union, Japan, and China—intersect and where these nations will compete or collaborate with each other. At the present time, it appears that each party hopes that a new balance of power will be maintained in Asia. The United States and China will no doubt play active roles in this region. To some Americans, China should be encouraged not only to serve as a counterweight to the Soviet Union but also to contain possible Japanese militarism. In any case, cooperation between the United States and China will be needed in constructing a new security system in Asia.

Second, with the signing of the INF Treaty, the United States and the Soviet Union have improved their bilateral relations and tensions have been eased. Against this general background, the two countries, having learned lessons from Vietnam and Afghanistan respectively, have a common desire to maintain an equilibrium in Asia. However, because their mutual suspicions are deeply rooted, each superpower will continue to regard the other as its chief adversary and threat. Despite the dramatic changes in Soviet foreign policies under Gorbachev, there are many uncertainties about the future of the Soviet Union, which will no doubt be a competitor for the United States even if it is no longer an adversary.

Third, in terms of security there are no direct and serious conflicts of interest between the United States and China, except over the issue of Taiwan. At present and in the foreseeable future, neither country will constitute a serious military threat to the other.

Fourth, although China and the Soviet Union normalized bilateral relations following Gorbachev's visit to Beijing, the improvement of their relations still will be limited because of historical and geopolitical reasons. Certainly, a resumption of the alliance of the 1950s is most unlikely. This becomes even clearer when one considers that the three obstacles, as seen from Beijing, have not yet been completely removed.

In short, with the normalization of Sino-Soviet relations, the strategic or Soviet factor no longer plays an important role as it did in the past, but it has not yet disappeared. The strategic triangle of the United States, the Soviet Union, and China has diminished in significance, but it is still functioning to a certain extent. The visit to China by President Bush, only 34 days after assuming office, provides the best illustration of current Sino-U.S. relations. This visit was naturally viewed by the Chinese as an important barometer of Sino-American relations. If both parties base their relations on mutual trust and mutual support and seek to reduce areas of friction, Sino-U.S. relations still will be better than either U.S.-Soviet relations or Sino-Soviet relations.

The Taiwan Issue

The Taiwan problem has been the key issue standing in the way of Sino-American normalization from the very beginning, and remains today a major obstacle to the smooth development of Sino-U.S. relations. Yet, without a complete resolution of the Taiwan problem, agreement was reached on a Joint Communique on December 15, 1978, announcing the restoration of Sino-U.S. diplomatic recognition, and bilateral relations since then have expanded considerably. The reason is that both the

United States and China have had common concerns about Soviet expansion in East Asia and elsewhere in the world, and this has tended to make the Taiwan problem a secondary issue. Because of this, there has been no serious friction between the two countries over the past few years. This does not mean, however, that the Taiwan obstacle has disappeared completely. The United States should not mistake China's realistic policy toward Taiwan as abandonment of principle and of its ultimate goal of reunification.

There have been fundamental differences over the Taiwan problem through the course of the Sino-U.S. normalization. Many Chinese assumed that normalization of Sino-U.S. relations would naturally and eventually pave the way to a solution of the Taiwan problem. At the initial stage of the opening to the United States, some top Chinese leaders, in their talks with American visitors, described the Taiwan problem as "a small issue" and seemed willing to "let it wait there for a time." In comparison with strategic considerations, the Taiwan problem was "small," but it still remained an issue; allowing it to "wait there for a time" could not be interpreted as giving up the goal of reunification of mainland China and Taiwan. As a matter of fact, China's senior leader Deng Xiaoping in his speech of early 1980 called for the fulfillment of three major tasks in the 1980s, one of which was reunification. On September 30, 1981, Chairman of the People's Congress of China Ye Jianying announced a nine-point policy regarding peaceful reunification of China. This was partly a reaction to the Reagan Administration's pro-Taiwan posture.

For some Americans, the greatest advantage to opening the door of U.S.-China relations was its impact on the Soviet Union. To China, U.S. administrations from Nixon to Reagan were reluctant in different degrees to abandon "old friends" in Taiwan. They wanted to maintain ties to both the PRC and Taiwan. Let us take a look at the record of U.S. policy toward the "two Chinas."

In the 1972 Shanghai Joint Communique, the United States acknowledged that "there is but one China and Taiwan is a part of China," but Washington did not recognize the government of the People's Republic of China as the sole legal government of China. In the Joint Communique of December 15, 1978, which announced that the two countries were establishing diplomatic relations with each other, the United States recognized the People's Republic of China as the "sole legal government of China." At the same time, the United States accepted the three conditions for normalization set by China: terminating diplomatic relations with Taiwan, abrogating the U.S.-Taiwan Mutual Defense Treaty, and withdrawing all remaining U.S. military personnel from Taiwan. But the question of continuing U.S. arms sales to Taiwan was put aside. On top of that, the U.S. Congress passed the Taiwan Relations Act soon after Sino-U.S. diplomatic relations were established. This was in fact a big step backward in the U.S. position toward the Taiwan problem. The August 17, 1982, Joint Communique set limits to future American arms sales to Taiwan, but the overall problem was not settled. These events indicate that the United States has never abandoned its policy of "one China, one Taiwan" or "two Chinas." This conclusion, reached by most Chinese, has been reinforced by Nixon himself, who notes in his memoirs that as late as August 1971, "We had . . . indicated our support of the concept of the 'two Chinas,' Chiang Kai-shek's Republic of China on Taiwan and the Communist People's Republic of China."[10]

Although the United States repeatedly stated, over a period of time, that it would not interfere in China's internal politics, most Chinese assert that the U.S. government has not only interfered but has legalized such interference in the form of the Taiwan Relations Act. As long as this legislation remains in effect, U.S. interference in China's domestic affairs cannot be considered over.

On August 17, 1982, shortly before the third Joint Communique was announced, Vice Premier Deng Xiaoping, in a meeting with American Ambassador Arthur Hummel, asked him to send a message to President Reagan to the effect that China values Sino-American relations and is ready to work together with the United States for a healthy development of bilateral relations, but that China is concerned about the cloud over Sino-U.S. relations caused by the Taiwan Relations Act. Deng Xiaoping also noted that even if this Act is not to be revised, the American President still has certain powers and flexibility over its implementation. He asked the Reagan Administration to give careful attention to this problem.

Unfortunately, even today there are still some influential people and institutions in the United States who assert that "the U.S.-China relationship rests on four pillars—the 1979 normalization of U.S.-PRC relations, the intergovernmental communiques of 1972 and 1982, and the Taiwan Relations Act,"[11] which in fact maintains the status quo of one China and one Taiwan.

---

[10]Richard Nixon, *RN: The Memoirs of Richard Nixon* (New York: Grosset and Dunlap, 1978), p. 556.

[11]Heritage Talking Points, "Bush's Trip to Tokyo, Beijing and Seoul," February 24-27, 1989.

The Taiwan issue must be solved in one way or another; if left unsettled for a long time or not settled satisfactorily, it will be a destabilizing factor in both the Taiwan Strait and the Asian-Pacific region, affecting not only Sino-U.S. relations but also Sino-Japanese relations. On this issue we should anticipate that there may be some changes and new contradictions or frictions over the Taiwan issue that may affect Sino-U.S. relations. For example, the tendency toward Taiwan independence may grow stronger in the near future: President Lee Denghui has adopted a flexible foreign policy to make Taiwan an independent political entity and bring about a *fait accompli* of "one China, two governments." A recent proposal suggested admitting Taiwan (and Hong Kong, South Korea, and Singapore) into OECD on the basis that OECD rules extend membership to "governments," not to "nations" or "states."[12] Such a proposal would clearly encourage the movement toward Taiwan independence and would be welcomed by Taiwanese authorities. The United States should approach this proposal with caution.

Furthermore, the Taiwan Relations Act affects the policies of other countries. Japan has already criticized China for adopting a strict policy on this issue with Japan but a lenient one toward the United States. ASEAN countries have shown a tendency to follow the U.S. lead with similar laws or regulations, which will in fact upgrade their relations with Taiwan. If Washington wanted to, it could keep its allies and friends from developing closer ties with Taipei. The objective of "peaceful reunification" adopted by China has been clearly stated, but to the Chinese, reunification is the precondition as well as the goal. However, some Americans talk only about a "peaceful settlement" with stress on "peaceful" but not on "settlement," let alone reunification. This obviously is not helpful to removal of the Taiwan obstacle from Sino-U.S. relations.

It should be made clear to all that China will never allow Taiwan to be independent. If an effort is ever made to treat Taiwan as an independent state, the result would seriously harm both Sino-U.S. relations and the prospects for peace and stability in the Asian-Pacific region. This is surely a development both Chinese and Americans would not want to see.

China's Modernization and Sino-U.S. Relations

In the years since early 1979 when Sino-U.S. diplomatic relations were reestablished and especially since the August 17, 1982, Joint

---

[12]Harry Harding and Edward Lincoln, "East Asian Laboratory," in John D. Steinbruner, editor, *Structuring American Foreign Policy* (Washington, D.C.: Brookings Institution, 1989), p.198.

Communique was announced, the nature of Sino-American relations has undergone important changes. Both the United States and China seem to have concluded that a sound bilateral relationship would not last long if it is based only on strategic—meaning anti-Soviet—considerations. Meanwhile, the two countries have managed to treat the Taiwan problem as a secondary issue, one that Chinese leaders gradually came to realize would not be solved quickly, not only for political but also for economic reasons. Instead, leaders in both countries have put emphasis on the importance of bilateral relations, especially economic cooperation.

At the end of 1978, the Third Plenary Session of the Eleventh Congress of the Communist Party of China adopted domestic reform policies, including the "three-step" development strategy designed by senior leader Deng Xiaoping, which set three goals: doubling the gross national product during the 1980s, doubling it again in the 1990s, and then attaining the level of a moderately developed country by the middle of the 21st century. This was immediately followed by the re-establishment of Sino-U.S. diplomatic relations. China's modernization program and the normalization of Sino-U.S. relations moved forward simultaneously, and their linkage was more than mere coincidence.

The Chinese government has decided to focus its effort on economic construction. An appreciation of China's tortuous history, and the experience of its opening to the outside world during the decade of the 1980s, have convinced the Chinese people that modernization must be the national goal and that it can never be achieved through isolation. The modernization program and the necessary reform and open policies that have been set in motion have been accepted by most of the Chinese people. This is indicated by the fact that not a single slogan was directed against the modernization program or the reform and open policies during the June 1989 turmoil in Beijing, and also by the fact that, even after the outbreak of the rebellion in Beijing, China's leaders are determined to proceed with their modernization programs and policies.

The ultimate success of China's modernization, of course, depends on the Chinese people themselves. But support from outside is also absolutely necessary; capital, technology, and management skills are badly needed. Therefore, when the Chinese talk about modernization, they naturally refer to the United States, the most advanced country in the world. Most of the Chinese people and their leaders believe that the improvement of Sino-American relations will be beneficial to China's modernization. America's advanced technology and management techniques can be adapted to Chinese needs, and its investment capital can provide an economic impetus, even though the two countries have different political and economic systems. Furthermore, a good relationship with the United States may influence other Western countries, which can also provide support for China's modernization.

In 1988, President Reagan asserted that "a strong, secure and modernizing China is in the interest of America."[13] It is also in the U.S. interest "to see a stable, developing China oriented toward pragmatic, reformist policies."[14] The healthy development of China's modernization program and the growth of China's economy would be a major contribution to the stability of the Asian-Pacific region, and this is a strategic interest of the United States. Some Americans even expect that economic reforms and an open policy would also provide a stimulus to the development of a market economy and political democratization in China, in conformity with the U.S. desire for the spread of democracy.

As a result of a common interest in China's modernization program, Sino-U.S. economic ties during the six or seven years before 1989 have expanded rapidly. Bilateral trade totaled 14 billion dollars in 1988,[15] up from only $5.2 billion in 1982. By the end of 1988, the United States had committed about $3 billion in direct investment in China through some 400 joint ventures, topping all other countries except the two areas of Hong Kong and Macao.[16] These trade and investment figures represent only a small share of U.S. totals, but from a long-term point of view, Sino-U.S. economic cooperation has great potential. If both sides make a sincere effort to develop it, such cooperation can be beneficial to American economic and strategic interests as well as China's modernization program. The two economies are mutually complementary rather than competitive. China will not become a competitor for the United States in the foreseeable future. On the contrary, as the United States faces an ever stronger economic challenge from Japan, China could be a valuable economic partner.

Good bilateral economic relations must be based on the principle of mutual interest and mutual respect. The Omnibus Trade Act of 1988 was the result of deterioration in the U.S. foreign trade situation and the rise of domestic protectionism. Even though the Act's thrust was directed mainly against Western Europe and Japan, China is also subject

---

[13]Ronald Reagan, *National Security Strategy of the United States* (Washington, D.C.: Pergamon-Brassey's, 1988).

[14]Robert A. Scalapino, "Trends and Implications in ASEAN-Major Power Relations," paper prepared for the International Roundtable, May 12-13, 1988, Bangkok.

[15]James R. Lilley's testimony, Hearings by Senate Foreign Relations Committee, USIA, East Asia/Pacific, Wireless file, April 13, 1989.

[16]Ambassador Winston Lord, Speech at the Federal Club of San Francisco, December 2, 1988.

to many of its protective provisions. As a latecomer, China is in a disadvantageous position in the competitive international market. The harmful effects of trade protectionism on China will not benefit the United States in the long run. China also hopes that Washington will cease using high-technology transfer as a lever to pressure China for political purposes.

China's modernization program can be a positive or a negative factor in Sino-American relations, depending on how it is handled by both parties. It would be unwise for China to become too dependent on the United States or any other country in pursuit of its goal of modernization. Nor would it be correct for Americans to think that the relationship will benefit only China—a one-way street, as some people put it, designed to help it with modernization. If the United States tries to use its economic assistance to China as a lever to bring about political democratization or a change in the economic system, the result would be counterproductive and could even make China close its door again.

Ideological Issues

State-to-state relations and foreign policy decisions are established and maintained on the basis of the national interest. Only by adhering to this principle can policies win comprehensive popular support and durable state-to-state relations be developed. Sino-U.S. relations are no exception. However, the national interest referred to here must abide by certain rules, the most important of which is that no country should safeguard its interests or realize its ambitions at the expense of other countries.

U.S. foreign policy has been a mixture of realism and idealism (i.e., ideology) in different forms at different times. After making some adjustments in the early 1980s, China has learned how to manage more wisely its national interests, economic modernization, and ideology and to weave these elements into a foreign policy which is supported by its people at home and is understood by other countries.

China and the United States differ in social systems and foreign policies but have had parallel national interests in many respects for the past twenty years and have handled their relations, until recently, in a responsible way. Common national interests led to President Nixon's visit to China and the first Sino-U.S. Shanghai Communique in 1972. The need to deal jointly with the Soviet threat forced the two countries to adopt realistic policies, casting aside ideological differences. As Henry Kissinger said, there are no permanent enemies, and U.S. judgment of other countries, including Communist China, should be based on their actions rather than their domestic ideology.[17]

The establishment of Sino-U.S. diplomatic relations in 1979 came almost simultaneously with China's adoption of the open policy aimed at the four modernizations.[18] The Carter Administration agreed to accept three conditions concerning Taiwan—to terminate diplomatic relations, abrogate the mutual defense treaty, and withdraw U.S. armed forces—and thereby took a big step forward in Sino-U.S. relations. This was a realistic policy designed to counter the Soviet Union. At the same time, China's foreign policy focused on an effort to secure a favorable international environment for its modernization program by emphasizing the importance of national sovereignty and security for all countries. Most Chinese and their government leaders recognize that state relations of different types have emerged since the end of World War II, but they contend that only those based on the five principles of peaceful co-existence have a lasting validity. They also believe that the state of China's relationship with other countries should not be predetermined by whether or not their social and economic systems and ideologies are similar. The Chinese government in fact observes this rule.

With the receding of the Soviet threat in recent years, U.S. strategic needs regarding China are now different from those in the 1970s. The rapid expansion of economic and cultural relations has diversified the contents of Sino-U.S. bilateral relations. "Idealism" has come to wield a larger influence over U.S. policy toward China. Its position as a superpower has also caused the United States to neglect the feelings and interests of other countries while attempting to impose its own system and values. For instance, the United States interfered with China's domestic politics on the issues of Tibet and family planning in the name of "human rights," thus injecting unpleasant factors in its bilateral relations with China and hurting the feelings of the Chinese people. Such action runs counter to Chinese interests as well as long-term U.S. interests, and the Chinese people find it very difficult to understand why the Americans engage in such open interference in other countries' affairs.

China's reform policies, begun at the end of 1978, have already achieved considerable progress in the economy and society, including the human rights sector. Since then and even in 1990, the Chinese people can

---

[17]Kissinger, *White House Years*, op.cit., p. 192.

[18]The four modernizations are modern agriculture, modern industry, modern science and technology, and modern national defense.

openly discuss such issues as civil rights and freedom, subjects that were taboo during the Cultural Revolution. Most Chinese intellectuals who lived through both periods would agree that progress in this area has been remarkable.

The seminar in commemoration of the 40th anniversary of the United Nations Declaration of Human Rights was held in Beijing from December 3 to 10, 1988. Assuredly, in the area of democracy and human rights in China there is a lot of room for improvement, and leaders, intellectuals, and the populace at large hold differing views on the issue. Further strengthening of human rights can only be achieved with the overall advancement of society and the legal system.

On the Tibetan issue, shortly after the Dalai Lama visited the U.S. Congress in September 1987, the Senate passed a resolution calling on the Reagan Administration to use high-technology as a bargaining chip to force China to "improve human rights in Tibet." On March 16, 1989, the Senate passed another resolution denouncing China's use of force against Tibetans and the violation of their human rights. The U.S. State Department correctly pointed out that Tibet is a part of China and kept a low profile on the handling of this issue. The situation in Tibet has improved, and Beijing hopes there will be no new interference in China's domestic affairs or damage to Sino-U.S relations. By trying to make a big issue out of events in Tibet, the U.S. Congress caused discontent among the Chinese people. Tibet is an integral part of Chinese territory: On that there can be no debate.

With regard to the criticism some U.S. Congressmen have made against China's family planning policy, most Chinese consider it is not even worthy of response. If the U.S. population totaled 1.2 billion, they might ask, what would Congress do? The one-child-family policy is a necessary choice for China; it is not only in China's best interest but it is also a contribution to a better world.

The United States may retain its own ideals and values, but it should not impose them on others. Former President Nixon once said that countries with different cultural backgrounds and at different stages of development need different systems. The United States should not use its own form of democracy to judge the governments of other countries. China and the United States have different political systems; each has its own national interests and is in a different stage of economic development. A system of democracy and human rights can only be attained when progress is made in a country's economy and society. Both China and the United States should focus their efforts on areas where their national interests are compatible rather than enlarging the gap between them through differences in ideology. In this way, stable bilateral relations can be nurtured over the long term.

Looking to the Future

Many Americans and Chinese were shocked and disappointed when the June 4th events in Beijing brought the United States and China close to a diplomatic rupture. Only three months before, when President Bush visited Beijing and held talks with Chairman Deng Xiaoping and other Chinese leaders, the top leaders of both countries expressed confidence in the great potential of improving Sino-American relations. Few persons could have foreseen the swift and unfortunate turnabout in Sino-American relations.

The American public and the U.S. Congress reacted swiftly and angrily at the events in Beijing. The Bush Administration immediately announced (June 5) that it had imposed sanctions against China suspending arms sales to and military exchanges with China. Two weeks later, on June 20, the White House announced further action, suspending high-level official contacts between the two governments.

In China, newspaper editorials and articles strongly criticized and protested foreign interference in China's internal affairs, especially by the United States. China's formal official reaction, however, was more moderate. For instance, at a June 22 press conference, the spokeswoman of the Foreign Ministry, besides protesting interference by the United States and other Western countries in China's internal affairs, advised foreigners to observe closely recent events in China and to adopt a calm and cautious attitude before drawing conclusions. It may surprise some that the Chinese government has so far not taken any major retaliatory measures against the United States.

Instead, the Chinese Communist Party (CCP) and government made public a number of official statements and speeches by leaders including Deng Xiaoping's June 9 speech[19] and his remarks on the development of the Four Cardinal Principles during the last ten years.[20] These statements were published primarily to show that China's reform and open policy remains unchanged, to explain to foreigners the real situation in China, and also to express China's willingness to strengthen Sino-

---

[19] *People's Daily*, June 28, 1989, p.1.

[20] *People's Daily*, June 24, 1989, p.1. The four cardinal principles: keeping to the socialist road, upholding the people's democratic dictatorship, leadership by the Communist Party, and Mao Zedong thought.

American relations on the basis of the Five Principles of Peaceful Coexistence.[21]

Following his initial strong actions, President Bush refused to impose further sanctions against China. Spouses of the officials working in the U.S. Embassy in Beijing and consulates in Shanghai and other cities soon returned to China, and U.S. Ambassador James R. Lilley attended ceremonies on different occasions in August 1989 in Tianjing and Shanghai.

In his address on regional cooperation delivered to the Asia Society in New York on June 26, 1989, U.S. Secretary of State James Baker stressed that human rights could not be the only factor in U.S. foreign policy decision-making. "The hasty dismantling of a constructive U.S. - Chinese relationship built up so carefully over two decades would serve neither our interests nor those of the Chinese people."[22] An important step was taken by the Bush Administration when it sent National Security Advisor Brent Scowcroft and Deputy Secretary of State Lawrence Eagleburger as special envoys to Beijing on December 9. Then, from early 1990 on, various steps were taken in return on the Chinese side, including the lifting of martial law first in Beijing on January 1 and later in Tibet on May 1; the release of 573 detainees who had been held since June 4, 1989; and finally, the decision to permit Fang Lizhi to leave the U.S. Embassy in Beijing and go abroad on June 25, 1990.

The above review of interactions between the two governments and the signals sent to each other during the past year shows clearly that there is still uncertainty about the future of the Sino-U.S. relationship, although there has been some improvement. To repair and to restore momentum to this bilateral relationship requires skillful efforts by leaders, politicians, and specialists of both countries.

It is difficult to predict the future of Sino-U.S. relations, but a cautious assessment may be given: This relationship, within the next two or three years, will neither deteriorate further nor improve rapidly. It is likely to remain largely unchanged.

The Sino-American relationship is indeed too important to be placed in jeopardy, as the events of the past forty years have demonstrated. The first twenty years of animosity and isolation resulted in two wars in Asia which deeply involved the United States and China and cost them both dearly. The friendly relations enjoyed by both parties throughout the

---

[21]*People's Daily*, August 13, 1989, p.1.

[22]James Baker, "Pacific Partnership—A New Mechanism," Address delivered to the Asia Society in New York City on June 26, 1989.

second twenty years, however, benefited the two countries a great deal, not only strategically but also economically. The United States is no longer facing challenges on two fronts, and China is now enjoying a comparatively peaceful environment in which the Chinese people can concentrate their efforts on modernization. Although China is an underdeveloped country, its economy is growing and its economic influence will inevitably increase. China's healthy, growing economy with its population of 1.1 billion is a stable factor in East Asia and the Pacific. Therefore, deterioration of the Sino-American relationship would not serve the best interests of the United States or China. National polls taken by the *Los Angeles Times* and ABC/*Washington Post* in mid-June 1989 indicated that 59 percent of those individuals questioned opposed halting trade with China, and 83 percent opposed severing diplomatic relations with China. These polls reveal that the American people are cognizant of the importance of Sino-U.S. relations. The Chinese sentiment is no doubt similar.

One cannot, however, expect to see the restoration of momentum in Sino-U.S. relations overnight. Ideological differences between the United States and China create a significant barrier to compromise. Consequently, it is extremely important when managing bilateral relations to reduce ideological differences as much as possible. China fully expects to adhere to the Five Principles of Peaceful Coexistence in its relations with the United States. In comparison with China, the United States has attached too much importance to ideology in its foreign relations. If the U.S. can refrain from imposing its ideological values on China, an improved bilateral relationship may result in the near future.

At present, the new Chinese leadership is trying to strike a balance between the four cardinal principles, and the reform and open policy. It is also stressing that the four cardinal principles, as the foundation of the country, must be adhered to unswervingly and consistently; and that the policy of reform and opening to the outside world, as the means for leading the country to strength and prosperity, must be implemented steadfastly. If the United States overemphasizes the ideological differences between itself and China, China will react strongly and tighten "ideology control" severely and, in the worst possible scenario, close its door and give up the policy of reform and opening to the rest of the world.

The most important principle to China in the Five Principles of Peaceful Coexistence is noninterference in each other's internal affairs. Americans are said to have short memories, but Chinese do not. The history of China is fraught with many bitter experiences of being invaded and subdued. The June events in Beijing have reminded the Chinese, especially the revolutionary veterans, of the "peaceful evolution strategy" conceived by former Secretary of State John Foster Dulles during the period of hostility between the United States and China.[23] It is extremely important that the U.S. Congress, as well as the Bush Administration, not attempt to interfere further in China's internal affairs. Intervention will only prove to be counterproductive, and it certainly is not the right way to keep China's door open.

Some Chinese argue that certain Western countries have been trying, by means of sanctions, to close the door of China which has gradually swung open during the past 20 years—an effort that will prove unsuccessful. At the same time, some Americans have suggested that a number of signals must be given by China to regain American confidence. At this point, what is needed is for the leaders of both governments to demonstrate enough courage and skill to break through the present stalemate in Sino-U.S. relations, just as Chairman Mao Zedong and President Richard Nixon did during a much more difficult time than we face today.

---

[23]In his testimony before the Senate on January 15, 1953, and on other occasions, Secretary Dulles spoke of the need to "liberate" people who were still under enslavement and to "stimulate evolution" within the Soviet-Chinese bloc. Those remarks have since been referred to by Chinese leaders as the "peaceful evolution strategy."

Sino-American Relations Since Tiananmen Square

by Robert L. Pfaltzgraff, Jr.

The June 4, 1989, massacre in Tiananmen Square, witnessed by the outside world on television, portrayed to a global audience the use of repressive power against a civilian population demanding for itself rights long enjoyed in countries such as the United States with democratically elected governments. The brutal repression of the Democracy Movement in China brought to the fore the long-standing American dilemma that has beset Sino-American relations since the rise to power of Chinese communism.

It had taken thirty years for the United States to bring itself to the point of opening the contacts early in the Nixon Administration that led a decade later to the establishment of full diplomatic relations with the People's Republic of China (PRC) at the end of 1979. Having opposed the Chinese communist quest for power in the years leading up to 1949, the United States had fought the Chinese People's Liberation Army after its intervention in the Korean conflict in late 1950. What had eventually changed American policy had not been any perception of a mellowing of the internal practices of the Beijing regime, but instead the need perceived by the Nixon Administration to bring China more fully into an emerging multipolar world. The rationale for an unfolding Sino-American relationship was set entirely within the geostrategic context. Discussion abounded in the United States about the need to play the "China card," by which it was assumed that the then deepening Sino-Soviet conflict opened important opportunities for American diplomacy. Specifically, the United States would be able to maintain, both with Moscow and Beijing, better relations than either could hope to evolve with the other. The deep rift between China and the Soviet Union conferred upon the United States important leverage with respect to both leading communist states, according to such reasoning. Set in the broadest geostrategic context, the American interest clearly lay in the preservation of a condition in which the largest state (the Soviet Union) remained politically at odds with the most populous state (China) so that neither, separately or together, could place itself in a position to dominate the vast Eurasian landmass.

Subordinated to such an approach to U.S. foreign policy was the question of the nature of the Chinese regime. Indeed, the use of one repressive government to counter another seemed to mitigate concern that might otherwise have troubled American consciences about the nature of Chinese communism. Hence, the Sino-American relationship proceeded on a course toward normalization, with President Nixon's historic visit to China in the midst of the Cultural Revolution which itself represented a vast suppression of modernizing elements in favor of totalitarian conformity. Only in the late 1970s did China emerge from what was widely described as tantamount to a civil war, which set back reform and modernization by at least a decade. In retrospect, the Tiananmen Square massacre and associated repressive measures against pro-democracy reformers elsewhere in China pale by comparison with the earlier protracted, destructive, and seemingly mindless brutalization of millions of people, including intellectuals and scientific groups, as well as the denunciation of leading political figures including Deng Xiaoping himself.

The process of Sino-American diplomatic normalization that proceeded from 1969 (at the beginning of the Nixon Administration) to the opening of full diplomatic relations a decade later (during the Carter Administration) is of interest for an analysis of Sino-American relations in the 1990s. Overall, the decade of the 1970s leading up to the U.S.-Chinese normalization was a period of deepening Soviet-American tensions, especially in the late 1970s culminating in the Soviet invasion of Afghanistan in December 1979. By the end of the decade and into the early 1980s, the United States had begun to forge with China a proto-alliance to oppose Soviet hegemonism. Both countries had a shared geostrategic perspective with respect to the ambitions and goals of Soviet global policy.

By 1989, however, the global geostrategic setting had changed dramatically. In the midst of the Tiananmen Square demonstrations, in May 1989, Mikhail Gorbachev visited Beijing, symbolizing the transformation of Sino-Soviet relations from hostility to accommodation toward normalization. Moscow had taken substantial political strides to meet China's preconditions for diplomatic normalization, including Soviet military withdrawal from Afghanistan, the removal of Vietnamese forces from Cambodia, and the dismantling of Soviet SS-20s targeted against China. In the Western media Gorbachev's visit to Beijing was all but overshadowed by images of Chinese students and workers gathered around the Goddess of Democracy in Tiananmen Square that bore a close resemblance to the Statue of Liberty.

Had a Soviet leader visited Beijing a decade earlier, such an event would have been justifiably interpreted as having profoundly unsettling implications for the Eurasian and Asian-Pacific geostrategic setting. In the changed circumstances of the late 1980s, however, China's geostrategic role, while by no means eliminated as a fundamental element in any Asian-Pacific balance, had become a less urgent consideration in American policy as the U.S. relationship with the Soviet Union entered a new phase with Moscow's mounting economic problems and Gorbachev's domestic challenges. Such was the setting in which the Sino-American relationship unfolded at the end of the 1980s and into the present decade, in which it became increasingly difficult, if no less necessary, for the United States to balance enduring geostrategic interests and the justified concerns about human rights highlighted by the Tiananmen Square massacre. In such context, therefore, it is appropriate to survey the respective interests of both sides in the Sino-American relationship in the 1990s.

The Chinese Perspective

From the Chinese perspective, relations with the United States remain important for a number of reasons. From the security dimension, the United States provides a useful counterbalance to the Soviet Union. While relations with the USSR are no longer nearly as tense as they once were, the two states have not restored the close relationship that they enjoyed with each other in the 1950s. Because Beijing shares a 4500-mile, often ill-defined, border with the Soviet Union, the potential for greater discord on territorial issues itself provides an incentive for China to maintain a relationship with the United States as a counterpoise to the Soviet Union. At the same time, the United States is an important trade partner for China. Sino-American trade exceeded $9 billion in 1988, whereas trade with the Soviet Union totaled a mere $3 billion. While the United States ranks as the second largest foreign investor in the PRC, China has made an important intellectual investment in the United States, with 40,000 Chinese students and scholars in the United States even after Tiananmen Square.

Despite the importance of the United States and China to each other, there remains an ambivalence in the relationship from both sides. In part, this is rooted in a long-standing Chinese xenophobia. As a result, despite China's interest in improving relations with the United States, Beijing also suggests that the capitalist West represents a danger. For example, in the aftermath of Tiananmen Square, the Chinese government has published articles on the Opium War. In an oblique reference to alleged Western imperialism and historic interference in Chinese domestic affairs, Chinese statements have reiterated that the Opium War was a Western effort to weaken China, with devastating consequences. The analogy to present circumstances is only thinly veiled. An article in *Renmin Ribao*, for example, which examined the Opium War, suggested: "We should learn a lesson from China's modern history. We should be aware that a backward country can be attacked by foreign powers and that modern China's weakness and poverty were mainly caused by the invasion of the capitalist powers."

The perceived need to continue to seek an appropriate balance between relations with the Soviet Union and with the United States, and the West more broadly, undoubtedly contributed to the Chinese decision to take further steps toward an improved relationship with Moscow in the wake of Tiananmen. Thus, just before Gorbachev's visit to Beijing, Li Peng had journeyed to Moscow for meetings from April 23 to 26, 1990. This first visit of a Chinese premier to the Soviet Union since 1964 resulted in agreements providing for science and technology cooperation, joint activities in space programs, mutual reductions in military forces on the Sino-Soviet border, an expansion of Chinese exports, and cooperation in nuclear power development.

Chinese links to the Soviet Union have steadily developed since Li Peng's Moscow visit. President Yang Shankun made a stopover in Leningrad in May, and General Liu Huaqing, vice chairman of the Central Military Commission, visited Moscow in June. A delegation of the National People's Congress visited the Soviet Union in July 1990. Then, on September 1, 1990, Soviet Foreign Minister Shevardnadze met with Zian Qichen, Chinese foreign minister, in Harbin, China. Again, while no joint or individual communiques were issued, there were nevertheless indications that the two states are proceeding to increase the channels of communication as a basis for improving relations. Their talks encompassed a variety of topics, such as the situation in Iraq, the Korean Peninsula, and Europe, as well as Cambodia. They also apparently discussed bilateral relations, including the need for a faster reduction of forces on the Sino-Soviet border, as well as the establishment of a Chinese Consulate General in Khabarovsk and a Soviet Consulate General in Shenyang. There were also indications that a state visit by President Qian to the Soviet Union will be forthcoming.

More important than the Sino-Soviet government-to-government links, however, has been the development of less formal ties, particularly at the economic level. For some Chinese provinces, such as Heilongjiang, Soviet demand for consumer goods has made the USSR their primary export market. To facilitate greater economic cooperation, the Foreign Trade Bank of the Soviet Union opened an office in Beijing and the Bank of China established an office in Moscow. Meanwhile, air service between Urumqi, China, and Alma Ata, USSR, and between Harbin and Khabarovsk has been initiated. Despite Moscow's economic failures, China continues to view the Soviet Union as a potential market and viable trade partner. In a recent issue of *Jingji Cankao (Economic Issues)*, it was suggested that China should look to the Soviet Union as a potential labor market. In particular, given the limited number of Soviet workers in Siberia and the Far East, it was suggested that cooperation should be increased between the two states leading to joint development of the region through Chinese manpower and Soviet technology. Such ties are likely to be strengthened as the transportation and communications infrastructure between the two states is improved.

An American Perspective

From the American perspective, relations with China are set within a context of ambivalence, but for different reasons than in the case of China's outlook toward the United States. The suppression of the Democracy Movement engendered a strong reaction of both sadness and anger in the United States. Long before Tiananmen Square, many Americans, including Members of Congress, had denounced violations of human rights in Tibet. In particular, the suppression of the Tibetan independence movement and the continued threat to the indigenous population by the deployment of Chinese military units into the region, as well as the desecration of local cultural sites, had spawned a strong reaction. The Tiananmen Square massacre dwarfed the Tibet issue, and the American response was swift. The killing or wounding of several thousand persons, recorded by the international media, could hardly have had consequences other than to turn American public opinion firmly against "business as usual" with the PRC. Indeed, in a *Los Angeles Times* poll taken soon after June 4, 75 percent of those questioned found China to be an unfriendly nation, a proportion almost exactly the reverse of results prior to the Tiananmen massacre.

These attitudes in turn were reflected in Washington's reaction to the repression of Beijing Spring. President Bush took action in four areas to express U.S. opposition to the Chinese repression: suspension of all government-to-government sales and exports of weapons; a halt in all visits between senior U.S. and Chinese military officials; general willingness to extend the visas of Chinese students in the United States; and the offer of humanitarian and medical assistance to those injured during the fighting.

In the United States Congress there was strong support for even greater action against the PRC government. Proposed responses ranged from complete economic sanctions to the withdrawal of the U.S. ambassador in protest and taking the issue of Chinese violations of human rights to the United Nations. However, President Bush, himself a former ambassador to China, expressed concern that policies leading to the international isolation of the PRC would ultimately prove counterproductive. As a result, by December 1989, he had dispatched National Security Advisor Brent Scowcroft, as well as Deputy Secretary of State Lawrence S. Eagleburger, on a secret mission to Beijing. While it was later described as an effort intended to keep the Chinese informed of the results of the Malta Bush-Gorbachev summit, its significance lay in the need perceived by the Administration to maintain high-level contact with Beijing.

In November 1989, former President Richard Nixon visited China. At that time, he voiced American opposition to the Chinese repression in Tiananmen Square and counselled the need for moderation. Given Nixon's status as the American president who initiated the opening of U.S. relations with the PRC, his words were at least heard, if not necessarily heeded. Equally important, he also underscored the continuing strategic importance of the U.S.-China relationship. His message was set within the context of the overall importance of China in the Asian-Pacific balance. Indeed, President Nixon implied that China shared broader economic interests with the United States (possibly against Japan) that might eventually replace or supplement the strategic concerns that had brought China and the United States together in the first place, i.e., the Soviet Union. This statement aroused controversy both in Japan and in the United States.

For many generations, the United States has vacillated between support for China and Japan. China has the advantage of its geostrategic position and nuclear weapons. In contrast, since World War II Japan has been a crucially important ally and trading partner of the United States. The Reagan Administration in some ways epitomized the dilemma facing American policy in East Asia. At first, the Administration supported China, promoting military ties and cooperation, including the establishment of joint intelligence posts (which are apparently still in operation, despite the Tiananmen Square massacre). Yet with the continued growth of Japan as an economic giant and the deepening links forged between Tokyo and Washington, together with massive Japanese investment in the United States, the U.S.-Japan relationship clearly constituted the dominant feature of the Reagan Administration's policy in the Asian-Pacific area.

As the Bush Administration weighs its relations with Beijing and Tokyo, it faces problems similar to those that confronted its predecessor. China remains an indispensable component of any emerging Asian-Pacific political-military balance, just as Japan is the crucially important high-tech economy and the leading U.S. trade partner outside North America. As former President Nixon implied, a sharpening of frictions between Japan and the United States, over trade issues, for example, would have the effect of heightening the importance of China to American policymakers. Similarly, the reverse would be the case with respect to American relations with Japan if, for example, China were to revert to a form of xenophobic introversion or to forge a tight relationship with a post-Gorbachev Soviet communist leadership. It is obvious that the enduring element of American interest in East Asia lies in a policy that avoids the need to make such a choice between China and Japan.

From the American perspective, then, China represents both a potential ally and a clear violator of basic human rights, just as Japan forms an economic competitor with a pluralistic political system based on protection of individual freedoms. Under present circumstances, China's ability to play the "Moscow card," threatening to tilt to the Soviet Union, is perceived to be limited. China itself appears to recognize that any such action would necessarily be at the expense of the technological and monetary resources that it desperately needs and which are only available from the West. At the same time, the United States views China as a player of some importance in the emerging security environment, including support for American policy in the struggle with Saddam Hussein.

Although Tiananmen Square continues to cast its dark shadow, Sino-American relations are being shaped by other factors as well that, taken together, provide a basis for a net assessment for the early 1990s.

Military Relations

Perhaps least changed as of late 1990 was the military relationship between the United States and China. The United States continued to maintain only minimal contact with the PLA, with no significant exchanges having been resumed between the two military establishments. In the aftermath of Tiananmen Square, there were no major ship or aircraft visits, nor any major arms sales to the PRC. The Chinese responded to such cutbacks in U.S. contacts by suspending one of the few major joint ventures in defense systems between the two states, the F-8-II project. This $550 million program would have involved Grumman Aerospace in the modernization of as many as 55 Chinese built F-8 jets with modern Western avionics and generally updated their capabilities. President Bush had been prepared to allow work to continue on this long-term project in order to preserve at least some basis for the resumption of military-strategic ties in the future.

The Chinese authorities, however, chose to cancel the program. Part of the reason for this action lay in escalating costs. Although the program was initially supposed to cost $10 million per plane, reports indicated that the final cost would have approached $12-$14 million, which apparently was much higher than China was prepared to pay. It also served to send a political message to Washington, particularly as the PLA is reported to be receiving a 15 percent increase in its budget over the next year. The implication was clearly that if the United States could scale back its relationship with China, the PRC could respond in kind. Toward that end, the PRC dispatched a high-level military delegation to Moscow that included General Liu Huaqing, vice chairman of the powerful Central Military Commission, as well as Aeronautics and Astronautics Minister Lin Zhongtang. They apparently concluded an agreement by which the Soviet Union will provide China with Su-24 ground attack aircraft and MiG-29 air superiority fighters. Moscow would also furnish technicians to help upgrade Chinese factories.

Like the decision to cancel the F-8-II, the motivation was not entirely political. Chinese military officials have long had an interest in acquiring Soviet equipment. Purchases of Soviet military systems would have the advantage of easing logistical burdens to a greater extent than would the acquisition of Western equipment, because China possesses large amounts of earlier generation Soviet systems. Moreover, Soviet equipment is generally cheaper and more suited to the austere conditions of the PRC. Nevertheless, the Chinese decision may also have been motivated by uncertainty about the future of Western military cooperation in light of the U.S. response to Tiananmen Square.

Economic Considerations

In the economic realm, China has recognized the need for Western capital and know-how for modernization. In the immediate wake of the Tiananmen Square massacre, the West cut off access to most loans and grants. On June 23, the World Bank announced that it would not consider China's request for $780.2 million in aid for seven projects. At the Paris Group of Seven summit in July 1989, the seven industrialized nations condemned the repression of the Democracy Movement and suspended most loans. They also requested the World Bank to postpone the processing of China's applications for new loans as well. At the same time, the Asia Development Bank postponed decisions on new loans worth some $1 billion, and the International Monetary Fund also suspended action on all loan applications from China. Private commercial banks, wary of the uncertain domestic political situation, also were reluctant to extend additional loans. China's tourist industry, a $2 billion a year source of foreign exchange, dwindled to a trickle, while new joint ventures also disappeared.

With the passage of time, however, attitudes have begun to change. In December 1989, the U.S. Export-Import Bank resumed the extension of credits to Beijing, and allowed the export of three satellites worth $300 million to China. Japan, France and West Germany also extended at least some loans to the PRC, although Japan was by far the most interested in re-establishing economic ties with China. By January 1990, the United States had further loosened its restrictions on loans to the PRC. The United States also chose not to oppose World Bank loans for "human needs," including $30 million for earthquake relief. In late 1990, at least nine World Bank loans, totaling some $1.7 billion, were under consideration, including a $350 million hydroelectric project.

Despite these developments, the prospects for external support for China's weakening economy remain limited. The July 1990 Houston summit of the Group of Seven did not reopen significant investment or loan sources. Neither France nor West Germany indicated any special interest in re-establishing economic links, while the United States merely declared that it would not oppose a renewed Japanese opening to the PRC. As a result, of the seven states only Japan has resumed credits, although these include one major agreement worth $5.3 billion over the next several years. Of the remaining states, however, none had restarted financial assistance by late 1990; meanwhile, some banks have cut China's short-term credit lines, and the international bond market has downgraded China's bond rating.

At the same time, China's application for admission to the General Agreement on Trade and Tariffs (GATT) has been placed in abeyance until 1991. This postponement was not based on Tiananmen explicitly, but was clearly linked to it. The working party of GATT states on membership, which was primarily composed of EC countries and the United States, indicated that China's introduction of more centralized economic planning, particularly price-fixing through state plans, together with its retreat from a market-oriented economy, made China's trading structure incompatible with GATT guidelines. The achievements of the past ten years of reforms have thus been seriously challenged.

Such actions form an additional burden for a Chinese economy already weakened following austerity measures imposed by the government in late 1988 and compounded by subsequent continuing political unrest. Most economic indicators have fallen off, including industrial production,

GNP growth rates, and employment levels. Only in the second quarter of 1990 did the economy show some improvement, but it remained unclear in late 1990 whether such a trend will continue. Moreover, China has begun once again to face rising inflation, which has the potential to ignite serious popular unrest (the Chinese have a great fear of inflation for they cannot forget the last days of the Kuomintang regime when the KMT yuan became virtually worthless). As of late 1990, moreover, trade and tourism continued to be a mere fraction of what they were prior to June 1989.

In 1990, China took two important steps toward strengthening its diplomatic-economic links in Southeast Asia. The restoration of relations with Indonesia and the probable establishment of links with Singapore are likely to result in the growth of trade between these states and China. Indonesia has already signed a new agreement to increase trade presently valued at $920 million per year. The Chinese have actively sought to expand their economic links with other Asian-Pacific states, and especially with the ASEAN states. Moreover, recent Chinese moves indicate a clear desire for increased South Korean investment and trade. At the same time, Beijing, in a reversal of past policy, has appeared amenable to Taiwan and Hong Kong membership in the Asian-Pacific Economic Cooperation Council (APEC), under what would be tantamount to a three-China policy. As APEC represents an OECD of sorts for Pacific Rim states, Beijing apparently considers it worthwhile to accept a certain political awkwardness in return for economic access and opportunities.

Diplomatic Relations

It is in the realm of diplomatic relations that Beijing has experienced the greatest successes since June 1989. One important aspect of this gradual re-acceptance into the world community was the American decision not to suspend China's most-favored-nation trading status. This move, which allowed China to continue exporting goods to the United States without fear of crippling tariff rates, was clearly in response to the Chinese quid pro quo of releasing dissident Fang Lizhi and his wife from their sanctuary in the U.S. embassy in Beijing. China has also succeeded in extending relations to a number of states in Southeast Asia and elsewhere in the third world. At the same time, it has been able to act as spokesman for the third world, even as it moves to assert itself in a broader global setting.

China's re-establishment of diplomatic relations with Indonesia constitutes a major step toward its emergence from any isolation resulting from Tiananmen Square. The two states had been estranged for a quarter-century since the Indonesian military uncovered Chinese plans for supporting a pro-communist coup in September 1965. For Beijing the link to Indonesia is particularly important in the area of Sino-American relations, since Jakarta has been especially interested in resolving the Cambodian issue, in which China has played a key role.

In Cambodia, the Chinese, by pressuring Pol Pot and the Khmer Rouge, have allowed the UN-sponsored peace process to move forward. This came after the American policy reversal on Cambodia in July 1990, namely, that the tripartite resistance coalition, which includes the Khmer Rouge, should not have occupied Cambodia's UN seat. The implication, of course, was that the Hun Sen Government in Phnom Penh, installed by the Vietnamese, should be given a larger role in the peace process. This is diametrically opposed to China's and ASEAN's position that the Vietnamese-backed regime is illegitimate. The American switch apparently caught ASEAN and the Chinese by surprise, and it was quietly opposed, at least initially, by both. By the end of September 1990, however, China had tacitly accepted this position as its own, and vowed not only to support a Supreme National Council that would include the Hun Sen regime, but also to curb the Khmer Rouge in the course of any peace settlement. China committed itself to doing so by limiting its assistance to Pol Pot, so long as Vietnam did the same toward the regime in Phnom Penh.

This modification in the Chinese position was important since the UN-sponsored initiative could have been scuttled by a Chinese veto in the Security Council. Beijing's willingness to accede to the UN effort furnished further evidence of a desire to reduce the diplomatic isolation China had suffered since 1989. In addition, it marked the beginning of a possible broader rapprochement between the PRC and the United States. Chinese willingness to support the American position presumably signaled that China was prepared to continue to cooperate with the United States in areas where their interests overlapped.

Such cooperation has also been exhibited in the course of the Iraq crisis. By supporting the various UN resolutions against Iraq and promising to abide by the sanctions, China has helped to bolster the coalition that opposes Iraq. It has also permitted the United States, in particular, to act in support of Saudi Arabia under the auspices of the United Nations rather than unilaterally. In so doing, the Chinese have ameliorated at least some of the tensions with the United States that were generated by Tiananmen Square.

PRC policy in the Gulf crisis has not simply been a response to American requests and interests. Part of the motivation no doubt lies in the desire to strengthen China's recently established diplomatic relations with Saudi

Arabia. Moreover, China has evolved a highly sophisticated diplomatic strategy in the United Nations where it remains a spokesman for the third world even as it supports certain superpower interests. In this case, China has succeeded in carving out an independent role for itself. One example lies in the Chinese delegation's interpretation of the wording in Security Council Resolution 665 (providing for the enforcement of sanctions against Iraq). While the United States held that the use of military power was permitted in enforcing the sanctions, and China voted with the United States to accept this resolution, the two states clearly differed as to the interpretation of the phrase "measures commensurate to the specific circumstances as may be necessary." Unlike the United States, Beijing held that it meant that no force was authorized. Despite this disagreement, China did not veto the resolution, nor did it voice any major protest when U.S. forces promptly stopped and boarded a number of Iraqi ships.

Similarly, China has attempted to reap the benefits of acting as "spokesman for the third world" in the Security Council. Toward this end, it has spoken out against superpower policies, including alleged American imperialism and the danger of a superpower condominium in a post-Cold War world. It has indicated uneasiness over U.S.-Soviet cooperation, based undoubtedly on the resulting loss of Chinese leverage over both Washington and Moscow that would ensue from such a development.

Prospects for the 1990s

In the years ahead, the Sino-American relationship will differ in several important ways from the 1980s before the tragic events in Tiananmen Square. First and foremost, the United States now has a more realistic understanding of the measures that the Beijing government is prepared to take in order to stifle dissent and to assure its own survival. By the same token, the Chinese leadership may have gained a greater insight into the limits of American willingness (or ability) to subordinate human rights to the needs of a geostrategic relationship. In the age of instantaneous images transmitted globally by television, the ability of any Chinese government to conceal repressive measures such as the Tiananmen Square massacre will continue to diminish. As such incidents are more widely seen by viewers on an international scale, it will become even more difficult for the United States to separate the geostrategic dimensions of its relationship with China from the Chinese leadership's treatment of dissidents.

Hence, the United States has an obvious interest in the evolution of China toward a more moderate, tolerant government committed to a freer press, a legal system based on protection of individual rights, and a market-oriented economy. In opposing such trends, China in the early 1990s stands at odds with the breathtaking transformation that has swept away communist regimes in Eastern Europe. The extent to which the present leadership can continue to resist these tides remains to be seen. Yet China is one of the world's great civilizations with a long and rich history that for centuries has stood against unwanted influences from the outside world. As such, China understandably will continue to resent and resist outside advice about how to manage its internal affairs. Moreover, its communist leadership, having witnessed the fate of its counterparts in Eastern Europe as well as Gorbachev's problems in the Soviet Union, will not willingly embark on policies whose effect would be to undermine its very existence. Paradoxically, the changes that have pointed up the intractable contradictions of communist regimes elsewhere and have a potential to spill over into China itself will make the Chinese political elite even less willing than otherwise might have been the case to accept major reforms.

Whatever its views of the domestic politics of China, the United States will find it necessary, as recent events in the Middle East illustrate, either to enlist China's cooperation or to forestall its opposition in regional conflicts in which both countries have interests. To the extent that the Iraq crisis is the first of such issues in which the United States will seek to assemble an international coalition possibly with United Nations support, China will be a factor to be considered. China will remain a major part of the Asian-Pacific political balance if only because of its vast size in territory and population. The United States will seek to preserve with China a strategic relationship in a world which in the years leading into the next century will feature an increasing number of regional power centers possessing advanced military capabilities and posing challenges to regional stability, as in the case of Iraq in the Middle East. We face potential nuclearization not only in the Middle East, but also in South Asia (India and Pakistan) and Northeast Asia (North Korea). Such eventualities in themselves will have important consequences for the power balances of their respective regions. They are the most obvious examples of contingencies in regions adjacent to China, involving security interests of the United States itself, and therefore of importance in the evolving context of Sino-American relations.

The United States and China have experienced widely differing phases in their relationship, from the hostility of the generation after 1949 to the amity of the early 1980s and the distinctive cooling of the months following Tiananmen Square. In their outlook, Americans have alternated between feelings of romantic affection toward China and things Chinese to implacable hostility. Conceivably, the next decade, as a result of the more recent past, will provide the setting for a more balanced Sino-American relationship based on the apparent need to reconcile U.S. geostrategic interests with our values about acceptable domestic political practices in a world of heterogeneity, conflict, and resulting challenges to national security.

BRASSEY'S (US), Inc.

List of Publications
published for the
Institute for Foreign Policy Analysis, Inc.

Orders for the following titles should be addressed to: Macmillan/Brassey's (U.S.), Inc., Front and Brown Streets, Riverside, New Jersey 08075 (toll-free telephone number: 1-800-257-5755); or to Pergamon-Brassey's, Headington Hill Hall, Oxford, OX3 0BW, England.

Foreign Policy Reports

Ethics, Deterrence, and National Security. By James E. Dougherty, Midge Decter, Pierre Hassner, Laurence Martin, Michael Novak, and Vladimir Bukovsky. 1985. xvi, 91pp. $9.95.

American Sea Power and Global Strategy. By Robert J. Hanks. 1985. viii, 92pp. $9.95.

Decision-Making in Communist Countries: An Inside View. By Jan Sejna and Joseph D. Douglass, Jr. 1986. xii, 75pp. $9.95.

National Security: Ethics, Strategy, and Politics. A Layman's Primer. By Robert L. Pfaltzgraff, Jr. 1986. v, 37pp. $9.95.

Deterring Chemical Warfare: U.S. Policy Options for the 1990s. By Hugh Stringer. 1986. xii, 71pp. $9.95.

The Crisis Of Communism: Its Meaning, Origins, and Phases. By Rett R. Ludwikowski. 1986. xii, 79pp. $9.95.

Transatlantic Discord and NATO's Crisis of Cohesion. By Peter H. Langer. 1986. viii, 89pp. $9.95.

The Reorganization of the Joint Chiefs of Staff: A Critical Analysis. Contributions by Allan R. Millett, Mackubin Thomas Owens, Bernard E. Trainor, Edward C. Meyer, and Robert Murray. 1986. xi, 67pp. $9.95.

The Soviet Perspective on the Strategic Defense Initiative. By Dimitry Mikheyev. 1987. xii, 88pp. $9.95.

On Guard for Victory: Military Doctrine and Ballistic Missile Defense in the USSR. By Steven P. Adragna. 1987. xiv, 87pp. $9.95.

Special Reports

Strategic Minerals and International Security. Edited by Uri Ra'anan and Charles M. Perry. 1985. viii, 85pp. $9.95.

Third World Marxist-Leninist Regimes: Strengths, Vulnerabilities, and U.S. Policy. by Uri Ra'anan, Francis Fukuyama, Mark Falcoff, Sam C. Sarkesian, and Richard H. Schultz, Jr. 1985. xv, 125pp. $9.95.

The Red Army on Pakistan's Border: Policy Implications for the United States. By Anthony Arnold, Richard P. Cronin, Thomas Perry Thornton, Theodore L. Eliot, Jr., and Robert L. Pfaltzgraff, Jr. 1986. vi, 83pp. $9.95.

Asymmetries in U.S. And Soviet Strategic Defense Programs: Implications For Near-Term American Deployment Options. By William A. Davis, Jr. 1986. xi, 71pp. $9.95.

Regional Security and Anti-Tactical Ballistic Missiles: Political and Technical Issues. By William A. Davis, Jr. 1986. xii, 54pp. $9.95.

Determining Future U.S. Tactical Airlift Requirements. By Jeffrey Record. 1987. vii, 40pp. $9.95.

Naval Forces and Western Security. By Francis J. West, Jr., Jacquelyn K. Davis, James E. Dougherty, Robert J. Hanks, and Charles M. Perry. 1987. xi, 56pp. $9.95.

NATO'S Maritime Strategy: Issues and Developments. By. E.F. Gueritz, Norman Friedman, Clarence A. Robinson, and William R. Van Cleave. 1987. xii, 79pp. $9.95.

NATO's Maritime Flanks: Problems and Prospects. By H.F. Zeiner-Gundersen, Sergio A. Rossi, Marcel Duval, Donald C. Daniel, Gael D. Tarleton, and Milan Vego. 1987. xii, 119pp. $9.95.

SDI: Has America Told Her Story to the World? By Dean Godson. Report of the IFPA Panel on Public Diplomacy. 1987. xviii, 67pp. $9.95.

British Security Policy and the Atlantic Alliance: Prospects for the 1990s. By Martin Holmes, Gerald Frost, Christopher Coker, David Greenwood, Mark D.W. Edington, Dean Godson, Jacquelyn K. Davis, and Robert L. Pfaltzgraff, Jr. 1987. xv, 134pp. $9.95.

Nicaragua v. United States: A Look at the Facts. By Robert F. Turner. 1987. xiv, 159pp. $9.95.

The Grenada Documents: Window on Totalitarianism. By Nicholas Dujmovic. 1988. xiv, 88pp. $9.95.

American Military Policy in Small Wars: The Case of El Salvador. By A.J. Bacevich, James D. Hallums, Richard H. White, and Thomas F. Young. 1988. ix, 51pp. $9.95.

The U.S.-Korean Security Relationship: Prospects and Challenges for the 1990s. By Harold C. Hinton, Donald Zagoria, Jung Ha Lee, Gottfried-Karl Kindermann, Chung Min Lee, and Robert L. Pfaltzgraff, Jr. 1988. xi, 100pp. $9.95.

Security Perspectives of the West German Left: The SPD and the Greens in Opposition. By William E. Griffith, Werner Kaltefleiter, Edwina S. Campbell, Jan Erik Surotchak, Tamah Swenson, Jacquelyn K. Davis, and Robert L. Pfaltzgraff, Jr. vii, 126pp. $9.95.

The INF Controversy: Lessons for NATO Modernization and Transatlantic Relations. By Jacquelyn K. Davis, Charles M. Perry, and Robert L. Pfaltzgraff, Jr. 1989.xii, 126pp. $9.95.

The South Pacific: Political, Economic, and Military Trends. By Henry S. Albinski, Robert C. Kiste, Richard Herr, Ross Babbage, and Denis McLean. 1989. xiv, 100pp. $9.95.

The South Pacific: Emerging Security Issues and U.S. Policy. By John C. Dorrance, Ramesh Thakur, Jusuf Wanandi, L.R. Vasey, and Robert L. Pfaltzgraff, Jr. 1990. xvii, 112pp. $9.95.

Books

Atlantic Community in Crisis: A Redefinition of the Atlantic Relationship. Edited by Walter F. Hahn and Robert L. Pfaltzgraff, Jr. 1979. 386pp. $43.00.

Revising U.S. Military Strategy: Tailoring Means to Ends. By Jeffrey Record. 1984. 113pp. $16.95 ($9.95, paper).

Shattering Europe's Defense Consensus: The Antinuclear Protest Movement and the Future of NATO. Edited by James E. Dougherty and Robert L. Pfaltzgraff, Jr. 1985. 226pp. $18.95.

Selling the Rope to Hang Capitalism? The Debate on West-East Trade and Technology Transfer. Edited by Charles M. Perry and Robert L. Pfaltzgraff, Jr. 1987, xiii, 246pp. $30.00.

Why the Soviets Violate Arms Control Treaties. By Joseph D. Douglass, Jr. 1988. xiii, 202pp. $32.00.

Ending a Nuclear War: Are the Superpowers Prepared? Edited by Stephen J. Cimbala and Joseph D. Douglass, Jr. 1988. x, 198 pp. $28.00.

INSTITUTE FOR FOREIGN POLICY ANALYSIS, INC.

List of Publications

Orders for the following titles in IFPA's series of Special Reports, Foreign Policy Reports, National Security Papers, Conference Reports, and Books should be addressed to the Circulation Manager, Institute for Foreign Policy Analysis, Central Plaza Building, Tenth Floor, 675 Massachusetts Avenue, Cambridge, Massachusetts 02139-3396. (Telephone: 617/492-2116). Please send a check or money order for the correct amount together with your order.

Foreign Policy Reports

Defense Technology and the Atlantic Alliance: Competition or Collaboration? By Frank T.J. Bray and Michael Moodie. April 1977. vi, 42pp. $5.00.

Iran's Quest for Security: U.S. Arms Transfers and the Nuclear Option. By Alvin J. Cottrell and James E. Dougherty. May 1977. 59pp. $5.00.

Ethiopia, the Horn of Africa, and U.S. Policy. By John H. Spencer. September 1977. 69pp. $5.00.

Beyond the Arab-Israeli Settlement: New Directions for U.S. Policy in the Middle East. By R.K. Ramazani. September 1977. viii, 69pp. $5.00.

Spain, the Monarchy and the Atlantic Community. By David C. Jordan. June 1979. v, 55pp. $5.00.

U.S. Strategy at the Crossroads: Two Views. By Robert J. Hanks and Jeffrey Record. July 1982. viii, 69pp. $7.50.

The U.S. Military Presence in the Middle East: Problems and Prospects. By Robert J. Hanks. December 1982. vii, 77pp. $7.50.

Southern Africa and Western Security. By Robert J. Hanks. August 1983. vii, 71pp. $7.50.

The West German Peace Movement and the National Question. By Kim R. Holmes. March 1984. x, 73pp. $7.50.

The History and Impact of Marxist-Leninist Organizational Theory. By John P. Roche. April 1984. x, 70pp. $7.50.

Special Reports

The Cruise Missile: Bargaining Chip or Defense Bargain? By Robert L. Pfaltzgraff, Jr., and Jacquelyn K. Davis. January 1977. x, 53pp. $3.00.

Eurocommunism and the Atlantic Alliance. By James E. Dougherty and Diane K. Pfaltzgraff. January 1977. xiv, 66pp. $3.00.

The Neutron Bomb: Political, Technical and Military Issues. By S.T. Cohen. November 1978. xii, 95pp. $6.50.

SALT II and U.S.-Soviet Strategic Forces. By Jacquelyn K. Davis, Patrick J. Friel, and Robert L. Pfaltzgraff, Jr. June 1979. xii, 51pp. $5.00.

The Emerging Strategic Environment: Implications for Ballistic Missile Defense. By Leon Gouré, William G. Hyland, and Colin S. Gray. December 1979. xi, 75pp. $6.50.

The Soviet Union and Ballistic Missile Defense. By Jacquelyn K. Davis, Uri Ra'anan, Robert L. Pfaltzgraff, Jr., Michael J. Deane, and John M. Collins. March 1980. xi, 71pp. $6.50. (Out of print).

Energy Issues and Alliance Relationships: The United States, Western Europe and Japan. By Robert L. Pfaltzgraff, Jr. April 1980. xii, 71pp. $6.50.

U.S. Strategic-Nuclear Policy and Ballistic Missile Defense: The 1980s and Beyond. By William Schneider, Jr., Donald G. Brennan, William A. Davis, Jr., and Hans Rühle. April 1980. xii, 61pp. $6.50.

The Unnoticed Challenge: Soviet Maritime Strategy and the Global Choke Points. By Robert J. Hanks. August 1980. xi, 66pp. $6.50.

Force Reductions in Europe: Starting Over. By Jeffrey Record. October 1980. xi, 91pp. $6.50.

SALT II and American Security. By Gordon J. Humphrey, William R. Van Cleave, Jeffrey Record, William H. Kincade, and Richard Perle. October 1980. xvi, 65pp.

The Future of U.S. Land-Based Strategic Forces. By Jake Garn, J.I. Coffey, Lord Chalfont, and Ellery B. Block. December 1980. xvi, 80pp.

The Cape Route: Imperiled Western Lifeline. By Robert J. Hanks. February 1981. xi, 80pp. $6.50 (Hardcover, $10.00).

Power Projection and the Long-Range Combat Aircraft: Missions, Capabilities and Alternative Designs. By Jacquelyn K. Davis and Robert L. Pfaltzgraff, Jr. June 1981. ix, 37pp. $6.50.

The Pacific Far East: Endangered American Strategic Position. By Robert J. Hanks. October 1981. vii, 75pp. $7.50.

NATO's Theater Nuclear Force Modernization Program: The Real Issues. By Jeffrey Record. November 1981. viii, 102pp. $7.50.

The Chemistry of Defeat: Asymmetries in U.S. and Soviet Chemical Warfare Postures. By Amoretta M. Hoeber. December 1981. xiii, 91pp. $6.50.

The Horn of Africa: A Map of Political-Strategic Conflict. By James E. Dougherty. April 1982. xv, 74pp. $7.50.

The West, Japan and Cape Route Imports: The Oil and Non-Fuel Mineral Trades. By Charles Perry. June 1982. xiv, 88pp. $7.50.

The Rapid Deployment Force and U.S. Military Intervention in the Persian Gulf. By Jeffrey Record. May 1983. Second Edition. viii, 83pp. $7.50.

The Greens of West Germany: Origins, Strategies, and Transatlantic Implications. By Robert L. Pfaltzgraff, Jr., Kim R. Holmes, Clay Clemens, and Werner Kaltefleiter. August 1983. xi, 105pp. $7.50.

The Atlantic Alliance and U.S. Global Strategy. By Jacquelyn K. Davis and Robert L. Pfaltzgraff, Jr. September 1983. x, 44pp. $7.50.

World Energy Supply and International Security. By Herman Franssen, John P. Hardt, Jacquelyn K. Davis, Robert J. Hanks, Charles Perry, Robert L. Pfaltzgraff, Jr., and Jeffrey Record. October 1983. xiv, 93pp. $7.50.

Poisoning Arms Control: The Soviet Union and Chemical/Biological Weapons. By Mark C. Storella. June 1984. xi, 99pp. $7.50.

National Security Papers

CVW: The Poor Man's Atomic Bomb. By Neil C. Livingstone and Joseph D. Douglass, Jr., with a Foreword by Senator John Tower. February 1984. x, 33pp. $5.00.

U.S. Strategic Airlift: Requirements and Capabilities. By Jeffrey Record. January 1986. vi, 38pp. $6.00.

Strategic Bombers: How Many Are Enough? By Jeffrey Record. January 1986. vi, 22pp. $6.00.

Strategic Defense and Extended Deterrence: A New Transatlantic Debate. By Jacquelyn K. Davis and Robert L. Pfaltzgraff, Jr. February 1986, viii, 51pp. $8.00.

JCS Reorganization and U.S. Arms Control Policy. By James E. Dougherty. March 1986. xiv, 27pp. $6.00.

Strategic Force Modernization and Arms Control. Contributions by Edward L. Rowny, R. James Woolsey, Harold Brown, Alexander M. Haig, Jr., Albert Gore, Jr., Brent Scowcroft, Russell E. Dougherty, A. Casey, Gordon Fornell, and Sam Nunn. 1986. xiii, 43pp. $6.00.

U.S. Bomber Force Modernization. Contributions by Mike Synar, Richard K. Betts, William Kaufmann, Russell E. Dougherty, Richard DeLauer, and Dan Quayle. 1986. vii, 9pp. $5.00.

U.S. Strategic Airlift Choices. Contributions by William S. Cohen, Russell Murray, Frederick G. Kroesen, William Kaufmann, Harold Brown, James A. Courter, and Robert W. Komer. 1986. ix, 13pp. $5.00.

Gorbachev's Afghan Gambit. By Theodore L. Eliot, Jr., 1988. vii, 19pp. $5.00.

Books

Soviet Military Strategy in Europe. By Joseph D. Douglass, Jr. Pergamon Press, 1980. 252pp. (Out of print).

The Warsaw Pact: Arms, Doctrine, and Strategy. By William J. Lews. New York: McGraw-Hill Publishing Co., 1982. 471pp. $15.00.

The Bishops and Nuclear Weapons: The Catholic Pastoral Letter on War and Peace. By James E. Dougherty. Archon Books, 1984. 255pp. $22.50.

Conference Reports

NATO and Its Future: A German-American Roundtable. Summary of a Dialogue. 1978. 22pp. $1.00.

Second German-American Roundtable on NATO: The Theater-Nuclear Balance. 1978. 32pp. $1.00.

The Soviet Union and Ballistic Missile Defense. 1978. 26pp. $1.00.

U.S. Strategic-Nuclear Policy and Ballistic Missile Defense: The 1980s and Beyond. 1979. 30pp. $1.00.

SALT II and American Security. 1979. 39pp.

The Future of U.S. Land-Based Strategic Forces. 1979. 32pp. $1.00.

The Future of Nuclear Power, 1980. 48pp. $1.00.

Third German-American Roundtable on NATO: Mutual and Balanced Force Reductions in Europe. 1980. 27pp. $1.00.

Fourth German-American Roundtable on NATO: NATO Modernization and European Security. 1981. 15pp. $1.00.

Second Anglo-American Symposium on Deterrence and European Security. 1981. 25pp. $1.00.

The U.S. Defense Mobilization Infrastructure: Problems and Priorities. The Tenth Annual Conference, sponsored by the International Security Studies Program, The Fletcher School of Law and Diplomacy, Tufts University. 1981. 25pp. $1.00.

U.S. Strategic Doctrine for the 1980s. 1982. 14pp.

French-American Symposium on Strategy, Deterrence and European Security. 1982. 14pp. $1.00.

Fifth German-American Roundtable on NATO: The Changing Context of the European Security Debate. Summary of a Transatlantic Dialogue. 1982. 22pp. $1.00.

Energy Security and the Future of Nuclear Power. 1982. 39pp. $2.50.

International Security Dimensions of Space. The Eleventh Annual Conference, sponsored by the International Security Studies Program, The Fletcher School of Law and Diplomacy, Tufts University. 1982. 24pp. $2.50.

Portugal, Spain and Transatlantic Relations. Summary of a Transatlantic Dialogue. 1983. 18pp. $2.50.

Japanese-American Symposium on Reducing Strategic Minerals Vulnerabilities: Current Plans, Priorities, and Possibilities for Cooperation. 1983. 31pp. $2.50.

National Security Policy: The Decision-Making Process. The Twelfth Annual Conference, sponsored by the International Security Studies Program, The Fletcher School of Law and Diplomacy, Tufts University. 1983. 28pp. $2.50.

The Security of the Atlantic, Iberian and North African Regions. Summary of a Transatlantic Dialogue. 1983. 25pp. $2.50.

The West European Antinuclear Protest Movement: Implications for Western Security. Summary of a Transatlantic Dialogue. 1984. 21pp. $2.50.

The U.S.-Japanese Security Relationship in Transition. Summary of a Transpacific Dialogue. 1984. 23pp. $2.50.

Sixth German-American Roundtable on NATO: NATO and European Security—Beyond INF. Summary of a Transatlantic Dialogue. 1984. 31pp. $2.50.

Security Commitments and Capabilities: Elements of an American Global Strategy. The Thirteenth Annual Conference, sponsored by the International Security Studies Program, The Fletcher School of Law and Diplomacy, Tufts University. 1984. 21pp. $2.50.

Third Japanese-American-German Conference on the Future of Nuclear Energy. 1984. 40pp. $2.50.

Seventh German-American Roundtable on NATO: Political Constraints, Emerging Technologies and Alliance Strategy. Summary of a Transatlantic Dialogue. 1985. 36pp. $2.50.

Terrorism and Other "Low-Intensity" Operations: International Linkages. The Fourteenth Annual Conference, sponsored by the International Security Studies Program, The Fletcher School of Law and Diplomacy, Tufts University. 1985. 21pp. $2.50.

East-West Trade and Technology Transfer: New Challenges for the United States. Second Annual Forum, co-sponsored by the Institute for Foreign Policy Analysis and the International Security Studies Program, The Fletcher School of Law and Diplomacy, Tufts University. 1986. 40pp. $3.50.

Organizing for National Security: The Role of the Joint Chiefs of Staff. 1986. 32pp. $2.50.

Eighth German-American Roundtable on NATO: Strategic Defense, NATO Modernization and East-West Relations. Summary of a Transatlantic Dialogue. 1986. 47pp. $2.50.

Emerging Doctrines and Technologies: Implications for Global and Regional Political-Military Balances. The Fifteenth Annual Conference, sponsored by the International Security Studies Program, The Fletcher School of Law and Diplomacy, Tufts University. 1986. 49pp. $2.50.

Strategic War Termination: Political-Military-Diplomatic Dimensions. 1986. 22pp. $2.50.

SDI and European Security: Enhancing Conventional Defense. 1987. 21pp. $2.50.

Strategic Defense: Industrial Applications and Political Implications. 1987. ix, 29pp. $2.50.

The Future of NATO Forces. 1987. xi, 37pp. $2.50.

Protracted Warfare—The Third World Arena: A Dimension of U.S.-Soviet Conflict. The Sixteenth Annual Conference, sponsored by the International Security Studies Program, The Fletcher School of Law and Diplomacy, Tufts University. 1987. xi, 37pp. $2.50.

Ninth German-American Roundtable on NATO: NATO Modernization, Arms Control, and East-West Relations. Summary of a Transatlantic Dialogue. 1988. vii, 68pp. $2.50.

Third International Roundtable Conference: East-West Relations in the 1990s—Politics and Technology. 1988. v, 48pp. $2.50.

Strategic Defense Initiative: The First Five Years. 1988. xiv, 90pp. $2.50.

Fourth International Roundtable Conference: The Atlantic Alliance and Western Security as NATO Turns Forty: Setting the Agenda. 1989. v, 54pp. $2.50.

Fifth International Roundtable Conference. The Atlantic Alliance in a Changing World: Maintaining Public Support. 1989. v, 51pp. $2.50.